THE BRITISH ACADEMY

The Composition of the Book of Isaiah

in the

Light of History and Archaeology

By

The Rev. Robert H. Kennett, D.D.

Regius Professor of Hebrew
and Fellow of Queens' College, Cambridge
Canon of Ely

The Schweich Lectures

1909

Wipf & Stock
PUBLISHERS
Eugene, Oregon

Wipf and Stock Publishers
199 West 8th Avenue, Suite 3
Eugene, Oregon 97401

The Composition of the Book of Isaiah in the Light of History and Archaeology
The Schweich Lectures 1909
By Kennett, Robert H.
ISBN: 1-59244-624-8
Publication date 3/22/2004
Previously published by The British Academy / Oxford University Press, UK, 1910

TO MY DEAR WIFE

מצא אשה מצא טוב ויפק רצון מיהוה:

PREFACE

THE three lectures contained in this volume, which were delivered in the summer of 1909 as the second annual course of the Schweich Lectures, are an attempt to tell in a simple way the story of the book of Isaiah, and are not to be regarded as a commentary upon the book. In many cases I have been content merely to indicate, by means of quotations, that view of the origin and date of particular sections which commends itself to me, and I have made no attempt to give in detail the arguments for the theory which I have thus suggested. Had I done this, the length of the lectures would have been enormously increased, and the amount of detail would, in all probability, have tended to distract attention from the points which I desire particularly to make prominent. I have intentionally abstained from multiplying references, especially when referring to uncontroverted facts which are not of vital importance to my argument. Although no discussion of the problems of the book of Isaiah can be altogether adequate which is not based on the original Hebrew, I have endeavoured, as far as possible, to keep before myself the needs of English readers.

I gladly avail myself of this opportunity of expressing my thanks to several friends for help which they have kindly given in the preparation and publication of these lectures. The Rev. C. H. W. Johns, Litt.D., Master of S. Catharine's College, and formerly Fellow and Lecturer of Queens' College, Cambridge, has not only allowed me to consult him on many occasions on questions of Assyriology, but has also read through the first lecture in manuscript. To my friend and colleague, Mr. A. B. Cook, M.A., Fellow and Lecturer of Queens' College, Cambridge, and Reader in Classical Archaeology, I am indebted for much information on Greek archaeology and religion. My obligation to him is indeed much greater than might be supposed from the number of cases in which his name is directly mentioned. My thanks are also due to the Rev. W. Emery Barnes, D.D., Hulsean Professor of Divinity, and to Mr. H. Loewe, who have read these lectures in proof. It is, however, only fair to state that I alone am responsible for the opinions here set forth. For the indexes I am indebted to the willing co-operation of my daughter.

ROBERT H. KENNETT.

Queens' College, Cambridge.
October 25, 1910.

CONTENTS

LECTURE I

THE NUCLEUS OF THE BOOK OF ISAIAH 1

LECTURE II

ENLARGEMENT OF THE ORIGINAL BOOK OF ISAIAH BY THE ADDITION OF PROPHECIES COMPOSED IN THE BABYLONIAN AND PERSIAN PERIODS 23

LECTURE III

MODIFICATION OF THE ENLARGED BOOK OF ISAIAH DURING THE MACCABAEAN PERIOD, AND ADDITION TO IT OF PROPHECIES RECENTLY COMPOSED 43

INDEX 87

PASSAGES OF SCRIPTURE QUOTED OR REFERRED TO . . . 92

THE COMPOSITION OF THE BOOK OF ISAIAH IN THE LIGHT OF HISTORY AND ARCHAEOLOGY

LECTURE I

THE NUCLEUS OF THE BOOK OF ISAIAH

AMONG the prophetical books of the Old Testament that which bears the name of Isaiah is generally held in the greatest reverence, not only among Christians but also among Jews. Here the former find in fullest measure the great conceptions which they believe to be 'fulfilled' in the life and work of Jesus Christ: here the latter are consoled with the comfortable words which can dispel the gloom of oppression and wrong; so that even those who walk in darkness have a sure and certain hope that they will see a great light. It is but natural, therefore, that there should be a general desire to gain some idea of the influences under which conceptions so noble came to be uttered. The zeal with which scholar after scholar has applied himself to the analytical study—the ' Higher Criticism ', as it is called—of the book of Isaiah is in itself an eloquent testimony to the greatness of the book. The present lecturer treads a path which has been trodden before him by many great scholars whom it would be an impertinence to praise. Right and left of him are piled up the accumulated stores of years of patient research. Other men have laboured, and, in so far as he has attained any fresh result, he enters into their labours. The work is, however, by no means completed. Many a theory, which at first sight has seemed to offer a satisfactory solution of the problems of the book, is found to be untenable in the light of a more microscopic examination. Again and again, perhaps, it will be found necessary to re-examine all the evidence available, before any theory of the composition of the book can be regarded as other than tentative.

This then must be the present lecturer's justification for choosing as the subject of these lectures a study which has been so thoroughly treated by some of the greatest Biblical scholars. His indebtedness to others is very great; probably it exists in many cases where he himself is unconscious of it. He has, however, endeavoured to form an independent judgement on the evidence before him rather than to catalogue or to discuss the opinions of others. In many cases, therefore, where he makes no claim to priority in setting forth opinions, he believes that he has arrived at such opinions by independent study, and that his conclusions have therefore this merit, that they may serve to confirm the opinions set forth by other people. It is accordingly unnecessary to attempt to give a bibliography of the book of Isaiah. There is, however, one name which every student of this book must hold in highest reverence—one which the very stones would cry out, if an English lecturer omitted to mention it—the name of Professor Cheyne. Of his stimulating and inspiring work the present lecturer cannot speak too gratefully. He feels indeed that he may claim Professor Cheyne as his teacher even where he ventures to differ from him in his conclusions. Among the foreign scholars who have contributed to the elucidation of Isaiah the foremost place must unquestionably be assigned to Bernhard Duhm.

Thanks to the labours of these and many other scholars there is much which at the present day may be taken for granted. To argue at length that the book of Isaiah is not all the work of Isaiah the son of Amoz, but a composite document, would be but to slay the slain. We no longer refer to the 'Deutero-Isaiah', unless it be in inverted commas. The careful study of the form of Hebrew prophecy, and the recognition of the fact that much which was formerly regarded as prose is in reality poetry, have demonstrated the patchwork character of much which was once considered homogeneous. The philological study of the Hebrew language combined with textual criticism has made it clear that originally prophets and psalmists arranged their ideas logically and consecutively, and that it was as impossible for them in speaking or writing as it is for ourselves to jumble up all three persons without giving some explanation of the change of person. Thus the canons with which the modern student begins his study of the Old Testament reveal to him at once many phenomena which escaped the notice of former generations. Difficulties in the way of the traditional views of Scripture, or even of the earlier critical views, leap to the eye at once. As the result of this new literary equipment it is now pretty generally recognized that the analysis of the book of Isaiah is a work of the utmost complexity, each of the main divisions of the book consisting of documents of different *provenance* and date. The problem therefore which now lies before us is to discover the origin and date of these documents—or perhaps they should rather be described as fragments—as well as the cause of their combination into one book. Here we require more than one class of *criteria*. Literary criticism, invaluable as it is in analysis, cannot afford us in such a book as Isaiah the same help which may be derived from it, for example, in the study of the Pentateuch; though even there it must be supplemented by historical criticism. Mere lists of words and phrases are not enough either to prove or to disprove the authorship of Isaiah. It would obviously be absurd to contend that the diction of a man whose ministry extended over not less than forty years must always have exhibited the same peculiarities. And as in such a case diversity of style would not necessarily prove diversity of authorship, so also similarity of language does not establish identity of authorship. For similarity between two passages may be due to the fact that the one is an *imitation* of the other, separated from it, perhaps, by a long interval of time; or it may be merely a doublet. In case of intentional imitation the later writer may bewray himself by some minor difference of idiom[1]; but it may frequently happen that no such clue is to be found.

In view of the great stress which is laid by some scholars on literary criticism alone, it may perhaps be well to give an illustration of this point from English literature. Let it be supposed that at the present day a German acquainted with the English language, but not familiar with English literature, found himself required to sort out and to arrange from internal evidence only a collection of tattered fragments of English similar to the collection of Hebrew manuscripts which Dr. Schechter brought to Cambridge from the Genizah of the Old Synagogue at Cairo. Let it be supposed that on one fragment he found the National Anthem as it was sung in the reign of her late Majesty, Queen Victoria, and, isolated, on another fragment this verse:

> Lips touched by Seraphim
> Breathe out the choral hymn,
>   'God save the Queen';
> Sweet as if angels sang,
> Loud as that trumpet's clang
> Wakening the world's dead gang—
>   God save the Queen.—

would any one blame him if he supposed the second fragment to be a continuation of the hymn on the first? And if he combined the two fragments together into one hymn, would mere literary criticism of such a hymn at a later date ever establish the fact that originally the first three stanzas were an utterance of most fervent loyalty to the throne, and the fourth an utterance of the fiercest republicanism? And, to apply this illustration, just as it was possible for Shelley to adopt in one sense a phrase and a form of verse which loyal Englishmen used in a different way, so it was possible for a Hebrew after the time of Isaiah to use the phrase, 'A remnant will return,'[2] in a sense

---

[1] Thus, for example, the author of Gen. vii. 8 shows himself to be the *imitator* of vii. 2, and not the same writer, by his use of the expression אֲשֶׁר אֵינֶנָּה טְהוֹרָה instead of אֲשֶׁר לֹא טְהוֹרָה הִיא.

[2] Cf. Isa. x. 21.

fundamentally different from that which it originally bore in the mouth of the prophet himself.

Literary criticism, therefore, is inadequate by itself to solve such a problem as that presented by the book of Isaiah, and must needs be supplemented by historical criticism; that is to say, it is necessary to inquire with reference to each section or fragment which literary criticism declares to be homogeneous, at what period *every one of its phrases would have a clear meaning*. It cannot be denied that there are some passages of which the text is corrupt past all restoration; in many cases, however, the corruptions, though they may cause uncertainty as to individual phrases, do not materially affect the general sense of the whole context. The textual critic of many portions of the Old Testament finds himself somewhat in the position of an architect who is called upon to restore a Gothic church which is grievously mutilated, and has lost every atom of tracery from its windows. Under such circumstances it is obviously impossible for the most skilful and learned architect to claim that the tracery which he inserts is of the same design as that which was originally there. But he can decide from other features of the building, such as the moulding of the arches, whether, for example, the tracery should be Decorated or Perpendicular; and the church as restored by him may be regarded as corresponding essentially to the design of the original architect. In like manner, to apply this illustration, in many cases where it is impossible to restore the exact *tracery* of a Hebrew prophecy or psalm enough remains to enable us to determine, so to speak, the order of architecture to which it belongs, and the purpose which it was intended to carry out. Stones may be chipped and broken; we may have 'churchwarden windows' instead of the original delicate tracery; but we can nevertheless see clearly the purpose of the building, and it will remain as a valuable witness to the history of the age in which it arose.

Historical criticism, therefore, is as essential as literary criticism; and to history must be added archaeology, which is indeed but a department of history. The consensus of literary, historical, and archaeological criticism forms a threefold cord which is not easily broken, however slight may be each of its several strands. In the course of these lectures our attention will be concentrated mainly on the witness of history and archaeology, though it may sometimes be necessary to consider problems of a more definitely literary character.[1]

---

[1] A convenient and valuable analysis of the book of Isaiah has been recently published by the Rev. G. H. Box. The present lecturer, however, considers that in many places a still more drastic analysis is necessary.

In an inquiry into the light which is thrown upon the book of Isaiah by history and archaeology two courses are open to us: either we may take the sections of the book in the order in which they are now arranged, and may examine each in the light of history; or we may first consider the history of Israel, and then look in the book of Isaiah for prophecies which exactly correspond with it. The first method is, perhaps, the most thorough and convincing, but it would take far too long for the time at our disposal; moreover, since the sections are not arranged in chronological order, it would be extremely confusing. It will be well for us therefore to follow the second method, and to consider briefly the history of Judah from Isaiah's time onward, dealing more particularly with those incidents to which passages in the book of Isaiah may be considered definitely to refer.

Of course, strictly speaking, it is only by a process of elimination that a passage can be *proved* to belong to a certain date, viz. by showing that it is inapplicable to the circumstances of any other time. But if history repeats itself, it seldom does so to such an extent that every word and phrase of a document written in one age will be equally suitable in another; and for practical purposes it will usually be enough to point out one period of history to which such a document really corresponds in all its parts.

One preliminary question, however, must be considered before we can profitably study the nucleus of the book of Isaiah (i.e. those passages which may plausibly be assigned to Isaiah the son of Amoz): in what way were Isaiah's prophecies originally published? Did the prophet deliver his message by the pen, or by word of mouth? And if the latter, did he himself commit his words to writing, or to what agency are we indebted for their preservation?

A full discussion of the literary characteristics of the passages generally assigned to Isaiah is impossible here; but it is not altogether arbitrary to state that it seems to be extremely improbable that the prophecies were committed to writing by the prophet himself, at least at the time when they were first composed. Had this been the case, we should be compelled to conclude that in the present book of Isaiah excerpts were made from the original documents without the slightest regard to their original connexion. Students of the Synoptic Gospels will indeed be willing to admit that an ancient editor treated his sources with the greatest freedom; but although there might be good reason for the dislocation of material, when, as in the case of the Pentateuch, it was necessary to combine into one two or more documents of different *provenance*, it is difficult to account for the tearing asunder of that which had been written by the author himself, and presumably was arranged as he intended it, in order to re-arrange it in a manner which obscures the connexion. The present lecturer trusts that he will not be understood as casting any doubt upon Isaiah's *ability* to write, if he states that in his opinion the evidence points to an oral stage in the transmission of his words. In fact Isaiah himself has given us a hint which is unmistakable. In chap. viii. 16, 17 we have his declaration that his prophetic teaching must be made as it were into a sealed parcel, laid up in his disciples as in a depository, in order that it may not be lost. The words, it is true, have been understood to mean that Isaiah determined to prepare a written record of his teaching, and to commit this as a sealed document to the custody of his disciples. But though there might have been some point in laying up in a sealed envelope a definite *prediction* until the time when the prophet declared that it would be fulfilled, it is difficult to see what purpose could be served by sealing up exhortations to repentance, teaching as to the will of Jehovah, warnings against superstition and sin. It is more natural to understand the words to mean that the prophet's teaching must be written on the fleshy tables of his disciples' hearts, where it might be known and read of all men.

If we may suppose that Isaiah's disciples preserved *orally* their master's teaching, just as the Apostles preserved that of our Lord, we have a clue to much that is otherwise puzzling. Our Lord and St. John the Baptist did not adopt an entirely new mode of life, but lived and taught as many prophets had lived and taught before them. And if, in what is universally admitted to have been a literary age, neither of these committed his words to writing, but 'sealed them up' among his disciples, it is still more probable that in an earlier age the prophets would have done the same. Indeed, in the case of the prophet Jeremiah it is clearly implied that it was only after he had been preaching for more than twenty years that he made any attempt to commit his words to writing; and it is probable that he would not have done so even then, had it not been for his desire to make his preaching known at court. Another indication that the prophecies of Isaiah were originally published orally is to be found in the poetical form of some of them. A poem can be easily learnt by heart and repeated, and in this way the prophetic teaching would quickly spread over the land.

That a written book of Isaiah did not exist for a considerable period after Isaiah's death is also made probable by the absence of any reference to it, or quotation from it, in the book of Jeremiah. True, arguments from silence are not conclusive, if taken alone, but it must be admitted that in the present instance the silence is difficult to account for on the supposition that a book of Isaiah's prophecies actually existed in the days of Jeremiah. Jerusalem as Jeremiah knew it, at all events at the beginning of his ministry, had not materially altered since the time of Isaiah, for, at any rate, the reforms of Hezekiah had been undone by Manasseh. The political and religious condition of Judah in the days of Jeremiah presented many points of similarity with the state of things with which Isaiah had been confronted; yet Jeremiah never points a lesson by reminding his hearers how his great predecessor's words were vindicated by the event; and when the prophet is on his trial, the precedent to which his advocates appeal is drawn not from Isaiah, but from Isaiah's comparatively obscure contemporary, Micah.

This, of course, does not imply that the teaching of Jeremiah presents no parallels with that of Isaiah, but only that there are no such *verbal* parallels as we should expect, if the words of Isaiah had been accessible in a written form, and had been generally regarded somewhat in the light of Scripture.

One other preliminary remark is necessary. It is probable that even the earliest collection of Isaiah's utterances has been considerably modified, and that only a portion of it has come down to us. It would seem that it has been subjected to somewhat the same sort of revision as that of which the book of Hosea shows unmistakable signs. Hosea, like Isaiah, evidently told his story to his disciples in the first person. But an editor of Hosea's prophecies has endeavoured, not very successfully, to give some account of the prophet himself, drawing his facts from the book of prophecies which lay before him; and in doing this he uses phrases which he has culled from the collection of Hosea's own words, but in a connexion in which we may feel pretty sure Hosea never used them. There is no reason to doubt that Hosea, when speaking of his unsuccessful struggle in his own home against primitive superstition, either actually applied to his wife the term אֵשֶׁת זְנוּנִים, or let it be inferred from his words that such a description would not be inapt, and, similarly, he may have spoken of his children as יַלְדֵי זְנוּנִים; but it is extremely improbable that he represented Jehovah as saying to him, 'Go, take thee a wife of whoredom, and children of whoredom'; for though one speaks of 'taking' a wife, one does not speak of 'taking' children. The awkwardness of the expression is due to the fact that a later editor is not telling the story in his own words, but is trying to use words and phrases of Hosea.

That a similar process has been carried out in the collection of the genuine prophecies of Isaiah is evident, for example, from such a passage as chap. vii. 2, where the words, ' and his heart was moved, and the heart of his people, as the trees of the forest are moved with the wind ', are obviously derived from a *poem*, probably composed on the situation by Isaiah himself, which, however, has not come down to us. Why any editor should have deliberately omitted from his book any prophecy which he had reason to consider genuine it is hard to say, and it would be rash to speak dogmatically. It may, however, be suggested as a possible explanation that long after Isaiah's death, probably at least as late as the time of the Exile, there arose a desire to know something of the *lives* of the prophets, and that an attempt was made to tell their story in somewhat the same manner as the stories of Elijah and Elisha in the book of Kings. If narratives of this kind existed, it may well be that in later times they took the place of the original prophetical books, or that later editors of the prophecies, having only mutilated manuscripts to deal with, were glad to make good to some extent the deficiencies by reference to them. In this way it would be possible to explain the introduction of narratives into the books of Isaiah, Jeremiah, Amos, and, to a less extent, Haggai.

One cause of the dislocation of prophecies is very evident, viz. the introduction of consolatory passages into denunciations and predictions of woe. To the close of the Canon the Jewish Church never entirely lost consciousness of the fact that it was a living Church. Its Scriptures were, so to speak, brought up to date from time to time to suit its needs. Those whose teeth were grievously set on edge by the sour grapes which their fathers had eaten, if they were to keep their faith in a God whose mercy endures for ever, required something more than the denunciations which had been addressed to their fathers. And even when the Canon was definitely closed, and the books of Scripture were regarded as too sacrosanct to be modified in any way, the principle which had guided the editors of the Scriptures regulated the practice of the Synagogue. As is well known, in reading Isaiah, the collection of the Twelve Minor Prophets, Lamentations, and Ecclesiastes it is customary for the reader after reading the last verse to repeat the last verse but one, in order to avoid closing with words of woe.

In like manner we perpetually find in the prophets comfort added to woe. The consequence in many cases has been not unlike what would result, if a painter were to take a picture of a storm in which the whole sky was painted black with clouds, and were to paint between the clouds bright patches of blue sky. Through almost his whole ministry Isaiah was called upon, so to speak, to paint storms : later prophets have painted blue sky and bright sunshine in the middle of the blackness. It is little wonder, therefore, if the pictures in their later form, regarded as landscapes, cause perplexity as to their precise meaning.

With these preliminary remarks we may pass on to consider the light which history throws upon the book of Isaiah. It is natural to begin with the circumstances of Isaiah's own time, although here the ground is for the most part familiar and well trodden.

Isaiah received his call, as he himself tells us, in the year that King Uzziah (or Azariah) died. Unfortunately the chronology of the book of Kings for the eighth century B.C. is contradictory and untrustworthy, and we are only on sure ground when the evidence of the monuments is clear and unmistakable. We may, therefore, for practical purposes, leave on one side the biblical chronology for this period, and base our dates on the evidence of the Assyrian inscriptions. Now Tiglath Pileser III, in describing a punitive expedition which he carried out in Northern Syria in the year 739 B.C. says, 'Nineteen districts of the town Hamath, together with the towns in their circuit, which are situated on the sea of the setting of the sun, which in their faithlessness made revolt to Azriau, I turned into the territory of Assyria; my officers, my governors I placed over them.'[1] Another fragmentary inscription of the same date which gives a list of princes who paid tribute to Tiglath Pileser apparently mentions Azariah of Judah (Azriau of Yaudi), but it would be rash to assume that he is spoken of as tributary, for the reference to him may be of the same character as that in the inscription just quoted. It is indeed asserted by some Assyriologists that Azriau of Yaudi has nothing to do with Azariah, King of Judah, but belonged to the north of Syria. Winckler's arguments on this point, however, scarcely appear conclusive. Assuming the identity of the names, we need not suppose either that Judah was the foremost military power in the west, or that the alliance between Hamath and Judah was directed against Assyria. Judah and the states of Northern Syria had good cause for alliance quite irrespective of Assyria. It is now becoming more and more generally recognized that throughout the greater part of the history of the two Israelite kingdoms, North Israel and Judah, the latter was tributary to the former. The pride of the Jewish editors, through whose labours the historical books of the Old Testament have assumed their present form, has, indeed, avoided direct mention of Judah's vassalage, though facts are recorded which are scarcely intelligible on any other hypothesis.

---

[1] See *Schrader*, vol. i, pp. 211 f., 243.

It was, no doubt, the desire to obtain independence which had induced Uzziah's predecessor, Amaziah, to undertake the war against Joash of Israel which had ended so disastrously; and it is clear from the language of Isaiah that the temper of the Judaean government at the end of Uzziah's reign had not materially changed since the time of Amaziah. And if the King of Judah was anxious to throw off the yoke of North Israel, the rulers of the Northern Syrian states may well have felt that the same yoke was a menace to them. For Jeroboam II had considerably enlarged his kingdom, of which the northern boundary had finally reached to 'the entering in of Hamath'. If we may suppose that Hamath and the neighbouring states had sought an alliance with Uzziah against North Israel, we can understand the motives which led to the Syro-Ephraimitic invasion of Judah. The faithlessness of the house of David having been manifested in the intrigues with Hamath which Tiglath Pileser made the excuse for his expedition in 739, the King of Israel felt it necessary, now that the danger from Assyria had come so near, to protect himself from the possibility of a stab in the back by removing the Davidic king from the throne of Judah. There is no reason to suppose that Tiglath Pileser really believed that there was any danger from Judah to be feared by Assyria. It was sufficient for his purpose that states over which he claimed suzerainty had given him an excuse for plunder by making an alliance with a foreign state.

But though the identification of Azariah of Judah with Azriau, King of Yaudi, if correct, throws a valuable sidelight on the political situation of the time, even without it the hints given by the books of Isaiah and Kings point to the conclusion that it was against North Israel that the warlike designs of Judah were directed. Throughout the long reign of Uzziah the resources of Judah, dissipated under Amaziah, had been carefully husbanded. The 'house of David' were on the watch for an opportunity which would enable them to carry out successfully the policy which under Amaziah had had such deplorable consequences. The rejection of the proposed identification of Azriau with Azariah would only deprive us of the exact date of Isaiah's call, which in any case cannot have been long before 740 B. C.

From Isaiah vii. 3 we learn incidentally that Isaiah had a son bearing the symbolical name *Shear-jashub* (i.e. 'A remnant will return'), who in 735 B. C. was old enough to accompany his father on the occasion of his celebrated meeting with Ahaz, and who therefore cannot have been born much later than 739 B. C. Since in 734 we find the prophet giving another son a symbolical name which, following the example of his older contemporary Hosea, he made the subject of an address to the people, it is only reasonable to suppose that *Shear-jashub* was in like manner the *text* of a sermon.

What, then, was the truth which Isaiah desired to impress upon the minds of his countrymen at the beginning of his ministry by the use of the pregnant phrase *Shear-jashub*? If we depend solely upon literary criticism, we must reply, arguing from chap. x. 22, that the prophet intended to teach that in a time of apostasy ' a remnant would return' to the God of Israel; and we must regard the words as a promise, or at least as a mitigation of a message of woe. But at his call Isaiah's view of the future was as gloomy as it well could be; for chap. vi. 13, which in the Masoretic text seems to imply a ray of hope, certainly cannot be claimed as an original utterance of Isaiah: it is extremely awkward in syntax, and moreover the last clause is wanting in the Septuagint.

If, then, the phrase *Shear-jashub* sums up a sermon of most gloomy prognostication, there can be very little doubt as to its original meaning, which must be '*Only* a remnant will return'; and the precise significance of the word 'return' may perhaps be illustrated by a reference to the words of Micaiah the son of Imlah (1 Kings xxii. 28) : ' If thou return in peace (*sc.* from battle), Jehovah hath not spoken by me.' The interpretation of the phrase *Shear-jashub* which best fits the circumstances of the time is ' Only a remnant will return from the war (*sc.* against North Israel) which the house of David is so wantonly provoking '. It is quite possible that, as the prophet Hosea at the close of his ministry, or a disciple of his, preached a sermon of consolation from the text *Jezreel*, which in its original (historical) associations had suggested nothing but woe, so the prophet Isaiah at the end of his ministry gave a new meaning to the phrase *Shear-jashub*, understanding it to mean that a remnant of the nation would turn with whole-hearted devotion to Jehovah ; but it must be admitted that the word ' remnant ' (שְׁאָר) implies that all those members of the nation not included in it will have perished : that is to say, the word does not mean ' a portion of Israel ', but ' all that remains of Israel ', *sc.* when the rest of the nation has been annihilated.

It would seem that the house of David were not checked in their schemes for political independence by the disaster which had overwhelmed their northern allies. For more than half a century Judah had been involved in no war of any magnitude, and the various little wars against the Philistines and others, if we may trust the book of Chronicles, had brought wealth into the king's exchequer. Isaiah alone seems to have had a clear conception of what must be the outcome of the warlike spirit which dominated Judah. To this early period of his ministry may be assigned portions of chap. ii. 6 ff. The passage, however, is not homogeneous; it contains more than one *hiatus*, and the great description of the day of the Lord is not necessarily originally part of the same discourse as ii. 6-8; though the mention of the ships of Tarshish suggests a date earlier than 735 B.C., when Elath, the only Judaean port, was taken by the allied forces of North Israel and Damascus.

While Isaiah was vainly endeavouring to convince his people that a little state such as Judah could not expect to maintain independence, the political situation in Palestine changed. The Palestinian states, which in their petty rivalries had been blind to the approach of the foe who threatened to destroy them all, had their eyes suddenly opened. When Northern Syria was subject to Tiglath Pileser, it was plain both in Samaria and in Damascus that the Assyrian's hand was being stretched out ever farther and farther, and that soon all the land would be held in his relentless grip. There seemed to be but one possibility of successful resistance, viz. that Israel and Damascus, and possibly the Philistines, should present a united front to the common foe. The one obstacle, however, to this policy was the attitude of the house of David. Blinded as they were by their own ambition to the Assyrian danger, their maxim was that North Israel's difficulty was Judah's opportunity. It is not impossible that Judah had already been guilty of some provocative act;[1] in any case it was clear that there could be no safety for North Israel in a war against Assyria until Judah had been thoroughly humbled. The result was the invasion of Judah in 735 B.C., or possibly as early as 736, by the combined forces of North Israel and Damascus. It was an epoch in Isaiah's ministry, and a careful consideration of the history of this time will enable us to sort out and to date a number of utterances which are otherwise most confusing. It is probable from Isaiah's stern words to Ahaz in chap. vii. 13 that the policy of the house of David which had resulted in the invasion of Judah by the allied forces had already been denounced by the prophet. Inasmuch as the parable of the vineyard (v. 1-7) appears to have been composed before Jehovah had broken down the wall of His vineyard, that is to say, before the country had actually suffered from invasion, it may be that it belongs to the period before the Syro-Ephraimitic war. By the vineyard, however, the prophet *may* mean Jerusalem rather than Judah, in which case the parable may possibly be later. Notwithstanding the statements in 2 Kings xvi. 5, Isa. vii. 1 it is doubtful

---

[1] Cf. Hos. v. 10. The passage, however, is too obscure to allow any argument to be based upon it.

whether Jerusalem itself was besieged at this time. There is no hint of a present siege in the story of Isaiah's interview with Ahaz. Possibly the invaders, knowing the strength of Jerusalem, and being unwilling to spend time on a long siege, desired to induce Ahaz to fight in the open. It is evident that the country districts of Jerusalem suffered grievously in the invasion, and by the capture of the port of Elath Judah's outlet to the sea was cut off.

It would seem that the panic-stricken Ahaz determined at once to appeal to Assyria, whereupon Isaiah, knowing of this determination, made a strong effort to induce him to abandon the idea of so disastrous a step. The invasion itself was but the natural result of the policy against which Isaiah had protested from the first, and of which he had declared that the consequence would be that only a remnant would return. Accordingly in the spring or early summer of 735 B.C. he sought an audience with the king outside the walls of Jerusalem. It was but natural that he should wish to remind Ahaz that the prediction which he had uttered some four or five years previously was in the way of being realized, and he accordingly took with him into the king's presence his little son *Shear-jashub* as the living text of the sermon which had originally been preached to deaf ears.

As we have noticed, the political situation had to some extent changed since Isaiah had received his call. The prophet now perceived clearly that the permanent danger to Judah was not from Ephraim (North Israel) and Damascus, for these powers were played out; but from Assyria. For the present, however, there was no need for panic. Even though Judah had suffered severely in the invasion, Jerusalem had no cause to fear. The smoking firebrands of Ephraim and Damascus would be burnt out before they could kindle a conflagration in Jerusalem. The proper policy of Ahaz for the present was to remain calmly on the defensive. Jerusalem could stand a siege for a considerable time, and Isaiah was convinced that within three years or so the power of the invaders would be broken. At the naming of *Shear-jashub* the prophet had probably affirmed that by the time the child reached a certain age the prediction implied by his name would be fulfilled. He now proceeded to give a similar sign, making use, however, for his purpose not of any particular child, but of a whole generation of children. It is not improbable that, as he talked to the king, his eye caught sight of one or more young women of marriageable age (העלמה)—perhaps they were spreading out, or gathering up, the clean linen in the fuller's field near by—who within a few months would probably be wives, and within less than two years mothers. An appropriate name for the firstborn child of any such young woman would, he maintained, be

Immanuel ('God is with us'): for by the time that the child would know what things hurt him and what things were good for him—that is to say within three or four years of the time when Isaiah spoke—Jerusalem would be delivered from the present danger, and it would be evident that God was with His people. Indeed, before the child would be able to say *Father* and *Mother*, Damascus and Samaria would be plundered by the king of Assyria.

It is evident from the very name *Immanuel* that Isaiah intended to *encourage* Ahaz to remain calmly on the defensive: it is therefore surprising to find, apparently connected with the same date (viz. the time when the child, or generation of children, would be barely old enough to refuse the evil and to choose the good), a statement that the staple food of the land of Judah will be curds and wild honey, because all the land of Judah is to be laid waste and cultivation is to cease. An explanation of the difficulty is probably to be found in the confusion with the Immanuel prophecy of another similar prediction spoken some nine months later.[1]

Isaiah's interview with Ahaz in 735 B.C. showed that the latter was not to be turned from his purpose in calling in the aid of the king of Assyria. Isaiah knew that by this policy Judah would only jump out of the frying-pan into the fire: it would be no gain to exchange the comparatively easy yoke of North Israel, or even of North Israel and Damascus, for the heavy yoke of Assyria. And considering the temper of the ruling classes in Judah, it was probable that the Assyrian yoke would not be accepted without a struggle sooner or later which would end in the absolute ruin of Judah. The plundering and looting of Jerusalem (of which he had had no fear in the Syro-Ephraimitic war) was now, Isaiah felt assured, near at hand. The prophet, however, had to deal with those who scorned his predictions so long as they were unfulfilled, and, when they were fulfilled, denied that they had been made. He accordingly wrote down on a tablet in the presence of credible witnesses, of whom one was no less notable a person than the chief priest of the sanctuary attached to the king's own palace, the words *Maher-shalal-hash-baz* (מַהֵר שָׁלָל חָשׁ בַּז, i.e. 'Plundering hastens, looting speeds'). Some nine months afterwards—probably early in the year 734—a son was born to Isaiah, on whom he bestowed as a name the words which he had written on the tablet. By this time Ahaz had

---

[1] The cause of confusion to the first editor of the book was doubtless the misunderstanding of viii. 4, which originally belonged to the *Immanuel* prophecy, but which in consequence of its containing the word שׁלל he supposed to belong to the *Maher-shalal-hash-baz* prophecy. This necessitated the transference to *Immanuel* of vii. 15, which originally referred to *Maher-shalal-hash-baz*.

LECTURE I

taken the fatal step of appealing to Assyria, and Tiglath Pileser was preparing to invade North Israel. As the name of his eldest boy had already furnished him with a text for a sermon, so Isaiah used the name of his second son to point the lesson which he was endeavouring to teach his people. The plundering of Jerusalem was rapidly approaching; its looting was at hand;[1] indeed, by the time that the child would be old enough to distinguish between things which hurt him and things which delighted him, his food would consist only of curds and wild honey; for, since cultivation would be at an end, and vineyards and cornfields would have become a common pasture ground, there would be no food for any one in Judah except wild honey and the milk of the cattle and flocks, which would be able to graze without let or hindrance on the hills which had once been renowned for their vineyards.

The statement of 2 Kings xv. 29 that 'in the days of Pekah, King of Israel, came Tiglath Pileser, King of Assyria, and took Ijon and Abel-beth-maacah and Janoah and Kedesh and Hazor and Gilead and Galilee, all the land of Naphtali; and he carried them captive to Assyria', is confirmed and amplified by Tiglath Pileser's own account of his expedition. He claims to have deported to Assyria 'the whole of the inhabitants of the land of Omri'; and we learn that Hoshea (who in the account of 2 Kings appears as the leader in a conspiracy against Pekah) was placed on the throne of Samaria by Tiglath Pileser after he had put Pekah to death. We can take the Assyrian king's boast that he has transported all the inhabitants of the land of Omri for what it is worth; but his statement is valuable as showing, what we should not have suspected from the biblical account, that not only Galilee and Gilead suffered in Tiglath Pileser's invasion, but the southern portion of the kingdom also. Indeed, the Assyrian army appears to have passed right through the kingdom of Israel and through the Philistine territory to the southern frontier of Palestine. Gaza was captured, and Hanno its king fled to Egypt. Well might Isaiah declare that his people, having forsaken the waters of Siloam that flowed gently, had brought into the land a river whose mighty onrush could never be checked.[2]

Having worked his will on Palestine, Tiglath Pileser turned his attention to Damascus. Since the Assyrian accounts represent expeditions against this kingdom in two successive years, 733 and 732, it is probable that Damascus was able to offer a more successful resis-

---

[1] This view of the original significance of the name receives some confirmation from chap. x. 6.
[2] Chap. viii. 7 f.

tance than North Israel. It was taken in 732, and Rezin was put to death. It was at this time that Ahaz was summoned to Damascus, among other tributary princes, to make his submission to the great king. Isaiah's predictions had been verified only too exactly; but even yet the ruling classes of Judah had not learnt the lesson which the prophet had endeavoured to teach. The heart of the people had indeed waxed fat, and their ears were heavy, and their eyes shut.

Of the years following 732 we have little information. It is probable that Ahaz continued subject to Assyria throughout his reign. He is mentioned by Tiglath Pileser in an inscription of the year 728 B.C. as paying tribute.

The Judaean politicians who had chafed at the suzerainty of North Israel were not likely to accept quietly the heavy yoke of Assyria; moreover, a powerful inducement to them to rebel was supplied by the policy of Egypt. It was becoming obvious that the real objective of Assyria was Egypt, and it was naturally the policy of the rulers of the latter to place one or more buffer states between their own country and their great rival. Accordingly any schemes of revolt against Assyria which might be formed among the Palestinian states were sure of finding sympathy and promises of help in Egypt. Even after 734 Palestinian politicians did not realize the full power of Assyria. In Samaria the disaster which had overwhelmed Galilee, and had affected in varying measure the whole of the kingdom of Israel, seems to have been regarded as a regrettable reverse which, however, would have no effect on the ultimate issue of the struggle. If the bricks had fallen down, the political building up of the future, it was contended, should be carried out in hewn stone; if the sycomores had been cut down, they should be replaced by cedars (Isa. ix. 9 f.). It was, of course, impossible to renew at once the struggle with Assyria, but upon the accession of Shalmaneser IV in 727 schemes of revolt began to be formed. In 725 Hoshea, relying upon Egyptian aid, refused his tribute, with the result that there was another invasion of the northern kingdom. The city of Samaria made a stubborn resistance, but was finally taken in 722 in the reign of Sargon, who had succeeded Shalmaneser during the siege. Sargon claims to have carried into captivity 27,280 of the inhabitants of Samaria.

Owing to the extreme uncertainty as to the chronology of the book of Kings, it is impossible to say with certainty in what year Ahaz was succeeded by his son Hezekiah. The latter is said to have reigned twenty-nine years (2 Kings xviii. 2), and if this is correct, we may perhaps calculate the year of his accession by reckoning backward from the reign of Josiah.

LECTURE I

It is generally admitted that Josiah came to the throne about 639 B.C., and, since his predecessor Amon reigned two years, 641 B.C. will be approximately the date of Manasseh's death. Inasmuch as there must have been a considerable number of people still living at the beginning of the Exile who remembered Manasseh's rule, there is a strong presumption that the number of years assigned to his reign is correct. If, then, we add fifty-five years to the date of Manasseh's death, we obtain the date of his accession and of the death of Hezekiah, viz. 696 B.C. Again, adding to this date twenty-nine years for Hezekiah's reign, we obtain 725 as the date of his accession, and 711, or thereabouts, as the date of his illness, which was believed to have occurred fifteen years before his death (2 Kings xx. 6, Isaiah xxxviii. 5). Since the embassy of Merodach Baladan, which in the biblical account is connected with Hezekiah's recovery, is in harmony with the known political circumstances of this time, we may, in the absence of more certain indications, accept 711 or 712 as its date.

The chief objection to this date is the statement that Sennacherib, who only succeeded to the throne of Assyria in 705, came up against all the fenced cities of Judah in the fourteenth year of King Hezekiah (2 Kings xviii. 13). If, however, we read 'the twenty-fourth' for 'the fourteenth' year we obtain the date 701, the year in which the Assyrian inscriptions place Sennacherib's campaign.

After the conquest of Samaria, Sargon was compelled to give his attention to Babylon, and the opportunity was not lost by the states of Syria and Palestine. Formidable revolts broke out in Hamath, Arpad, Simyra, Damascus, and Samaria, and further south Hanno, King of Gaza, formed an alliance with Egypt. In 720 Sargon returned to the west, and after dealing with the revolt of which Hamath was the centre he advanced against the allied forces of Egypt and Gaza. A battle took place at Raphiah in which the Assyrians were victorious. Sargon claims to have received tribute from Pharaoh, King of Egypt, as well as from some Arabian kingdoms. It may, however, fairly be doubted whether Egypt really acknowledged Assyrian suzerainty at this time. We need not necessarily suppose that what the Assyrian kings describe as tribute would have been so described by those who are said to have paid it. In like manner, when Sargon styles himself 'the subjector of the land of Judah', we need not infer that any fighting had actually taken place in Judah. Hezekiah's unresisting submission must needs be described in terms which implied greater prowess on the part of the Assyrian king.

For some years Sargon had no further difficulty in the west, and consequently in the absence of Assyrian armies schemes of revolt began again to be formed. In an inscription of the year 711 Sargon describes an expedition which he dispatched against Ashdod in which he mentions Philistia, Judah, Edom, and Moab as having formed an alliance with Pharaoh, King of Egypt. It is to this expedition that Isa. xx. 1 refers. Since Sargon does not mention any fighting in Judah, it is probable that Hezekiah saved himself by a timely submission. Merodach Baladan's embassy to Hezekiah probably preceded this campaign against Ashdod.

In the years 710 and 709 Sargon was engaged in Babylonia against Merodach Baladan. The latter was driven from his throne, and Sargon became master of Babylonia. It is not impossible that Isaiah's prediction in chap. xxxix. 7 in its original form referred to Sargon's capture of Babylonia, though in the form in which we have it it obviously refers to Nebuchadnezzar.

Sargon died in 705, and the Philistine states, now that the rod which had smitten them was broken,[1] began to dream of independence. For some time Hezekiah appears to have held aloof from any political combination. It was not long, however, before the opportunity of regaining independence appeared too good to be lost. On the one hand Merodach Baladan, who had been supplied with troops by the King of Elam, reoccupied Babylon, and Sennacherib's attention was claimed by the revolt in that region; on the other hand Tirhakah of Ethiopia was extending his power, and was encouraging the Palestinian states to rebel against Assyria. Apparently all the southern states of Palestine, and possibly the northern also, had at this time entered into a confederacy against Assyria. In this Hezekiah seems to have been the moving spirit, the only dissentient being Padi, King of Ekron, whose subjects accordingly deposed him and sent him as a prisoner to Hezekiah. Probably Isaiah was one of the few who realized the futility of the whole scheme, and the poetical prophecy in chap. v. 26-30, as well as the graphic account of the advance of the Assyrian army of which only a mutilated fragment remains in chap. x. 28-32, is plausibly assigned to this period.

After subduing the Babylonian revolt and carrying out a campaign in the mountains north of Elam, Sennacherib turned his attention to the west, where he carried out an expedition in the year 701. He first subdued the Phoenician cities of the north, and then advanced to the

---

[1] The prophecy in Isa. xiv. 29 ff. has been plausibly assigned to this date, in which case we must correct the heading in ver. 28, reading מֶלֶךְ אַשּׁוּר for הַמֶּלֶךְ אָחָז. The text, however, has suffered considerably, and has apparently been modified at a later date. There is no evidence for the supposition that Ahaz subdued Philistia, unless we are to find it in 2 Chron. xxviii. 18!

LECTURE I

Philistine plain. In the course of the expedition he received the submission of the kings of Ammon, Moab, and Edom. Ashkelon, as well as a number of tributary towns, was besieged and taken. At Eltekeh Sennacherib was met by troops from Egypt and Ethiopia which had advanced to the help of the Philistines. He claims to have defeated them, and they apparently retired from the country. Sennacherib thereupon besieged Ekron, which he captured. He then proceeded to assert his power over Judah. Forty-six strong cities of Judah were captured and added to the kingdoms of Ashdod, Ekron, and Gaza. Sennacherib claims also to have besieged Hezekiah in Jerusalem— though he does not mention the capture of Jerusalem—to have imposed an increased tribute, and to have received from Hezekiah an enormous amount of gold and silver and treasures, as well as the king's own daughters and a number of slaves.

The reconciliation of Sennacherib's account of this campaign with the biblical account is a matter of extreme difficulty. It must, however, be admitted that the Assyrian king's description is not marked by lucidity: he claims, for example, to have received the submission of Ammon, Moab, and Edom, but does not tell us at what stages in the campaign their submission was made. Moreover, the absence of any mention of the taking of Jerusalem is noteworthy, and it may be inferred that the amount of gold and of treasures which Hezekiah sent to Sennacherib was by way of buying him off.

It is by no means impossible, therefore, that the account given in the book of Kings is substantially correct, viz. that Hezekiah made his submission to Sennacherib before an Assyrian army had advanced on Jerusalem, and that the enormous amount of gold and silver and treasures, which both the inscriptions and the Bible represent Hezekiah as paying to the King of Assyria, was dispatched from Jerusalem at this time. Thereupon it would seem that Sennacherib, having come to the conclusion that he had let Hezekiah off too easily, sent a detachment of his army to besiege the city, but that the siege was suddenly raised in consequence of an outbreak of plague in the main army. If Sennacherib relates events in the order in which they happened, it is difficult to see why Ammon, Moab, and Edom should have made their submission *before* Hezekiah ; and if the siege of Jerusalem ended in the capture of the city by the Assyrians, Hezekiah's continued occupation of the throne is quite inexplicable.

Moreover, if Sennacherib's demand for the unconditional surrender of Jerusalem involved a breach of faith on his part, the attitude of Isaiah is more easily understood. That he should have opposed revolt against Assyria is in harmony with all that we know of his principles. In later times the prophet Ezekiel (chap. xvii. 15, 16) considered the oath of allegiance which the King of Judah had taken to Nebuchadnezzar to be binding, and we have no reason to suppose that Isaiah's view would have been more lax in the similar case of Hezekiah. But when Sennacherib had put himself in the wrong, the prophet who had uttered to Ahaz the prophecy of *Immanuel* was perfectly consistent in giving similar encouragement to Hezekiah. The Assyrian had been indeed the rod of Jehovah's anger; but the rod had fulfilled Jehovah's purpose of chastisement, and the time had come when it should be broken. Isaiah had seen the evil which intense arrogance had brought on Palestinian kings: it was not difficult to believe that like arrogance on the part of the King of Assyria would be followed by a similar result. The year 701 B.C. is memorable as the year when against all seeming probability Isaiah foretold the downfall of Sennacherib, and his prediction was verified. It is reasonable to suppose that it was at this period that he prevailed upon Hezekiah to attempt a thorough-going reformation; for the prophet's chief opponents, who at an earlier period had scouted him, were now discredited by the falsification of their predictions. Another reason for putting Hezekiah's reforms and the destruction of the brazen serpent after 701 is the recrudescence of superstition in the age of Manasseh. If the chronology adopted above is correct, it was only four or five years at most between the reformation carried out by Hezekiah and the reaction under Manasseh.

It is thus obvious that during the whole period of Isaiah's ministry the shadow of Assyria lay dark upon his path. The loss of forty-six fortified cities, besides many small towns and villages and the capture of 200,150 men, was a blow from which the kingdom of Judah never recovered. Even if Sennacherib's force was compelled to retire without compelling Jerusalem to surrender, there is no evidence that Judah was freed. The deliverance only meant that Jerusalem did not undergo the horrors of a capture, and that Hezekiah was not impaled or flayed alive. There is no indication that from the first appearance of Isaiah to the time when we lose sight of him any event took place in Judah which would awake a cry of victory.

Of the prophecies in the book of Isaiah which may reasonably be assigned to Isaiah the son of Amoz many cannot be dated with any certainty. The denunciations of the ruling classes (i. 10-17, 21-23, iii. 14, 15. v. 8-10, ix. 13 ff., xxii. 15-23, xxviii. 7-22) are shown by a comparison with the book of Micah to be as appropriate in the reign of Hezekiah as in the reign of Ahaz. The various references to the ruin of Judah and Jerusalem (e.g. i. 7-9, iii. 6-9) are perhaps more naturally understood of the events of 701, but they *may* belong to an earlier date. The 'woes' may be spread over the whole of Isaiah's ministry. That no argument as to date can be drawn from the existing position of sections, which are, moreover, in many cases made up of quite disconnected fragments, may be seen by a comparison of, for example, i. 9 with i. 10. In ver. 9 the names Sodom and Gomorrah are used as examples of a terrible *destruction*; in ver. 10 as examples of great *wickedness*.

It is impossible to read the book of Isaiah without being impressed by the comparative absence of direct attacks upon the superstitions of his time. With the exception of chap. i. 11-14 there is in those portions of the book which may plausibly be assigned to Isaiah himself no denunciation of the sacrificial system against which such a splendid protest is made in Mic. vi, and on which still later Jeremiah poured out his scathing sarcasm (Jer. vii. 21); no denunciation of the abominations committed at the high places which had called forth the eloquence of Hosea; no denunciation of the sacrifice of the firstborn son of Ahaz; and this in a book which bears the name, and undoubtedly preserves some of the teaching, of a man whose horror of idolatry and superstition was so great that under his influence even the brazen serpent which Moses had made was broken up! Can it be that that venerable idol was destroyed before Isaiah had publicly lifted up his voice against it? Surely the earnest exhortations, the teaching which Isaiah sealed up among his disciples, must have contained reference to these things. We can only account for their omission on the supposition that we have mere fragments of Isaiah's prophecies. Whether they were omitted by intention or accident it is impossible to say definitely. If, however, we may assume a fairly long *oral* stage in the transmission of Isaiah's teaching, so that it was not actually committed to writing till the reforms of Josiah had become recognized as law, we may perhaps account most easily for the omission. To condemn the worship of the brazen serpent or human sacrifice to people who were not addicted to either would have been superfluous. It may well be that much of the teaching of Isaiah was forgotten because it had no direct bearing on the conditions of a later age. One thing, however, could never be forgotten, viz. Isaiah's declaration that, though the Assyrian was the rod of Jehovah's anger, the Assyrian himself had no such view, but was actuated entirely by insensate ambition which must lead to his punishment. Such teaching could not but bring comfort to those who had but to substitute *Chaldaean* for *Assyrian* in order to apply it to their own case. It was perhaps in this way that Isaiah, the stern preacher of repentance, came to be regarded as the comforter of his people. If this was so, we can understand why words of comfort spoken during the Exile were added to his book, which thus became the model for subsequent comforters. And when the book of Isaiah had once come to be regarded as a book of national consolation, the tendency, which we find in other books of the prophets, to interpolate comfort into woes would here be specially prominent. There would be no desire to retain at all cost the *ipsissima verba* of the prophet, but only to edify the Church; the interest which Isaiah's words possessed for later ages was not historic, or antiquarian, but religious.

LECTURE II

ENLARGEMENT OF THE ORIGINAL BOOK OF ISAIAH BY THE ADDITION OF PROPHECIES COMPOSED IN THE BABYLONIAN AND PERSIAN PERIODS

For upwards of seventy years from the time that Isaiah disappears from our view the forces at work in Judah appear to have been altogether reactionary. The reformation which Hezekiah had carried out had gone beyond the popular conscience. It is not improbable that many who were sincerely desirous of some measure of reform stood aghast at the iconoclasm which destroyed the brazen serpent. Hezekiah's son and successor, Manasseh, who was a mere boy when he ascended the throne, was in the hands of the reactionary party, and continued, either from conviction or from motives of policy, to set his face ruthlessly against the reformers, reintroducing the practices which in his father's reign had been made illegal. From a religious point of view Manasseh's reign was a time of the deepest gloom, nor was the political horizon any brighter. Esar-haddon, who succeeded Sennacherib 680 B.C., claims to have received tribute from Manasseh among the kings of the Palestinian states, and also from various Phoenician and North Syrian kingdoms. Esar-haddon carried out a campaign in Egypt in 670, when Memphis was taken. The introduction of colonists into Samaria mentioned in Ezra iv. 2 is probably to be dated about this time. There *may* have been some insurrection in the province of Samaria which was the immediate cause of this policy. Certainly the *glossator* who added the latter half of ver. 8 of Isa. vii imagined that sixty-five years after the conversation of Isaiah with Ahaz, i. e. about 670 B.C., something happened which deprived the people of what had been the northern kingdom of any right to consider themselves a nation. Ashur-bani-pal, who succeeded in 668, carried on the war in Egypt, and received the tribute of the kings of the seacoast, including Manasseh. The statement in Ezra iv. 10, which there is no reason to doubt, that Asnappar (i. e. Ashur-bani-pal) transferred a number of people from the eastern portions of his dominions to the province of Samaria, shows that during his reign Assyria was in close touch with Palestine. It is probable, therefore, that Josiah, who succeeded to the throne of Judah in 639 B.C., reigned as vassal of the Assyrian king, and took an oath of allegiance to him.

Ashur-bani-pal died in 626, the year in which Jeremiah began to prophesy, and under his successors the empire declined rapidly. At this time the Scythian hordes were pouring into Western Asia, and were exercising a disintegrating influence on the unwieldy Assyrian empire, which had been extended solely for purposes of plunder, and had never been welded together into a political whole. It is probable that the foe from the north whom Jeremiah had in view at the beginning of his ministry was none other than the Scythian. Whether Judah actually suffered from the Scythian invasion is doubtful. The danger at any rate came very near, for the Scythians advanced into Philistia as far as Ashkelon, and Scythopolis (the Greek name of the city known in earlier times as Beth Shan) perhaps implies that they effected a settlement in the plain of Jezreel.

At the same time that the Scythians were pouring into the empire from the north, other barbarous Aryan tribes, the *Umman-manda* as they are called by Nabonidus, of whom the Medes appear to have been a branch, were harassing it on the east. Nor were these the only foes. On the death of Esar-haddon his younger son Shamash-shumukin had succeeded to the throne of Babylon. For some years he acknowledged the suzerainty of his elder brother Ashur-bani-pal, but finally with the support of the King of Elam and a king of Arabia he revolted. The revolt was put down by Ashur-bani-pal, but the power of Babylon was not broken. Finally, Nabopolassar, who became king in 625 B.C., found an opportunity of establishing his independence in the invasion of Assyria by the Medes, with whom he formed an alliance, marrying his son Nebuchadnezzar to the daughter of Cyaxares, the Median king. The combined armies of the Medes and Babylon attacked Nineveh, which fell about 606 B.C.

It is conceivable that, even if Nineveh had not been thus attacked, the fall of the great empire might have come about through Egypt. In 608 Pharaoh Necho, son of Psammetichus I, determined to win back the Asiatic dominion of Egypt. He was vainly opposed at Megiddo by Josiah, who, presumably, was acting as vassal of the King of Assyria, and he advanced victoriously as far as the Euphrates. For three years Judah was compelled to accept the suzerainty of Egypt, but in 605 a battle was fought at Carchemish between Nebuchadnezzar and Necho, with the result that the latter was utterly routed, and was obliged to retire from Asia.

Nebuchadnezzar was unable immediately to press his advantage; for, while he was pursuing Pharaoh, his father, Nabopolassar, died in Babylon, and it was necessary for him to return home. As soon as he had been installed as king, however, he exacted the submission of Syria and Palestine, and Jehoiakim, who had been placed on the throne by Pharaoh, was compelled to take an oath of allegiance to him.

LECTURE II

It was not long before schemes of revolt again began to be mooted in the west. After paying tribute for three years Jehoiakim withheld it. According to 2 Kings xxiv. 2 Nebuchadnezzar at first sent to Jerusalem an army composed in part of levies raised from the neighbouring kingdoms, Syrians, Moabites, and Ammonites being specially mentioned. It must be admitted, however, that the statement of the book of Kings is somewhat vague; moreover, it is difficult to reconcile it with the fact that in Jer. xxv (which apparently contains the gist of prophecies uttered by Jeremiah about the year 604, though these prophecies have scarcely been preserved in their original form) it seems to be implied that *all* the Palestinian states are confederate against the Chaldaeans. It is at any rate clear from Jer. xl, xli that at the time of the murder of Gedaliah Ammon was opposed to the Chaldaeans. In 597, however, while the siege of Jerusalem was in progress, Nebuchadnezzar himself took the command of the Babylonian troops. Jehoiachin, who had succeeded to the throne of Jerusalem three months before, surrendered, and together with the queen-mother and many members of the royal family was taken to Babylon. Nebuchadnezzar is stated to have plundered the temple of all its treasures, and to have taken away from Jerusalem all the nobility and gentry as well as all the fighting men. This is almost certainly an exaggeration, but Jerusalem evidently suffered grievously at this time. The numbers of the captives are variously given in the Old Testament. 2 Kings xxiv. 14 mentions 10,000 captives exclusive of the artisans; 2 Kings xxiv. 16 (which Stade rightly regards as taken from a different source) mentions 8,000 in all; while Jer. lii. 28 (which, notwithstanding the fact that the year of the siege of Jerusalem is called the seventh year of Nebuchadnezzar instead of the eighth, as in 2 Kings xxiv. 12, must refer to the same occasion) gives 3,023.

Jehoiachin's uncle Mattaniah, who now took the name of Zedekiah, was placed on the throne of Jerusalem by Nebuchadnezzar, who first exacted from him a solemn oath of allegiance (Ezek. xvii. 13-16). For some years Zedekiah quietly accepted his position; but in the year 588 B.C. Psammetichus II of Egypt, who had reigned for six years, was succeeded by his son Apries (Hophra), and the latter, unhappily for Judah, at once revived the policy of Necho, and began to instigate the Palestinian states to rebel. Jerusalem was besieged by the army of Nebuchadnezzar early in the year 587. An Egyptian army which came to the aid of the Jews was repulsed by Nebuchadnezzar, and Jerusalem fell in the summer of 586. Zedekiah, who had fled, was taken prisoner and carried to Riblah (2 Kings xxv. 6), where Nebuchadnezzar was at the time; his sons were put to death before his eyes; he himself was blinded and carried captive to Babylon. A month later the Chaldaean general burnt the palace at Jerusalem and the temple attached to it, as well as all the larger houses, and razed to the ground a great portion of the wall. A second time a large number of the inhabitants of Jerusalem were transported to Babylon, those who remained in the city being apparently the poorest of the poor. A considerable portion of Zedekiah's army continued to elude the Chaldaeans, and for a time found refuge beyond the Jordan; and doubtless a number of well-to-do, if not noble, families remained in other parts of the kingdom. According to Jer. lii. 29 the number of those carried away to Babylon at this time was 832.

The fact that the Chaldaean general appointed as governor of Judah a Jew named Gedaliah the son of Ahikam is in itself sufficient proof that the country was not depopulated. Nor can it be argued from Gedaliah's residence at Mizpah instead of Jerusalem that the latter city was destitute of inhabitants, although it is probable that for some time after the termination of the siege it was scarcely habitable. We know that it had endured the worst extremities of famine (2 Kings xxv. 3), and in such cases famine is accompanied by pestilence. Those who could live elsewhere must have been glad to do so.

In course of time the circumstances of Judah began to improve.[1] Gedaliah, evidently acting on the authority of Nebuchadnezzar, promised an amnesty to all fugitives if they would settle down quietly in the country and accept the rule of the King of Babylon; whereupon many who had fled to the neighbouring lands returned to their homes, and cultivation was resumed. Unfortunately for the peace of Judah a number of guerrilla bands still remained in the country, whose generals were deterred from making their submission, partly, perhaps, through doubt as to the good faith of Nebuchadnezzar, partly through the vain hope that resistance to the Chaldaeans might even yet prove successful. Gedaliah would probably have succeeded in inducing these generals to disband their forces, for the majority of them were evidently disposed to accept his promise, had it not been the policy of the surrounding states to hinder the pacification of Judah. The King of Ammon in particular knew that as soon as Judah was utterly crushed his own country would be brought under the yoke of the King of Babylon (cf. Ezek. xxi. 18 ff.). At his instigation one of the Judaean generals, Ishmael by name, treacherously murdered Gedaliah

---

[1] Perhaps it was during the governorship of Gedaliah that Jeremiah or one of his disciples composed the prophecy which has come down to us in various forms in Jer. xxiii. 5 ff., xxxiii. 14 ff., which is referred to in Zech. iii. 8, vi. 12, and imitated in Isa. xi. 1.

at Mizpah, together with his Chaldaean bodyguard and a number of Jews who were associated with him. The remainder of the population of Mizpah Ishmael carried off, intending to take them to Ammon. He was, however, pursued by the other generals, who intercepted him at Gibeon and released his captives. Ishmael himself, however, contrived to escape to Ammon.[1] Thereupon the other generals and their men, together with the people whom they had recovered from Ishmael, fearing the vengeance of the Chaldaeans, fled at once to Egypt, where other Jews and perhaps refugees from the province of Samaria had probably found an asylum, thus forming the nucleus of the very considerable Jewish population which we know from the Mond papyri to have been settled in Egypt in the fifth century B.C.

The date of the murder of Gedaliah is uncertain, for though the biblical account at first sight implies that it took place in the same year as the destruction of Jerusalem, viz. 586 B.C., two months (cf. 2 Kings xxv. 8, 25) would appear to be barely sufficient for the events recorded in Jer. xl. It is therefore possible that a considerable time elapsed between the appointment of Gedaliah and his murder, and it may be that the *third* transportation of Jews to Babylon in the year 581 B.C. mentioned in Jer. lii. 30 was the immediate consequence of Ishmael's action.

Still, however, Judah was not depopulated. The story of Gedaliah shows that, at all events as late as 586, there was a large *fighting* element in Judah, and this alone should be sufficient to disprove the old idea that *all* the Jews were taken to Babylon. In any case Mizpah and the Jerusalem district would have suffered most. There is no evidence that Southern Judah was equally affected, though it is obvious that apart from damage inflicted by the Chaldaeans the whole country must have suffered to some extent in the absence of any effective government.

By these events in the year 581 B.C. the population of Judah which had survived the wars and famines of the last sixteen years had been divided into three distinct parts, of which one remained in Judah itself, one, consisting of most of the aristocracy and the priesthood, had been carried to Babylon, and one had voluntarily settled in Egypt. All three parts were destined in later times to exercise an influence on the fortunes of the nation.

Of the Egyptian dispersion until recent years there was no evidence apart from the Bible. It is now certain, however, from the various papyri discovered in the neighbourhood of Syene (Assouan) that a very

---

[1] Perhaps it was this agreement between Ammon and Ishmael that so embittered the prophets against that country. Cf. Ezek. xxv and also Deut. xxiii. 3.

large number of Jews were settled in that district in the fifth century B. C. Indeed, in the Elephantine papyri it is claimed that since the time of Cambyses (c. 525 B. C.) the Jews of that place have had a temple where sacrifices have been offered to Jehovah (Yahu). It is certainly surprising to find a Jewish colony so far south at such an early date. The book of Jeremiah (chaps. xliv, xlvi) implies that at the time when the historical chapters were written the Jews who had fled to Egypt were settled mainly in the north, especially in the neighbourhood of Tahpanhes (i. e. the modern Tel Defenneh, about 25 miles south-west of the ruins of Pelusium), Noph (i. e. Memphis, about 10 miles south of modern Cairo), and Migdol (probably in the north-east not far from Pelusium). Pathros (Upper Egypt) is also mentioned in Jer. xliv as containing settlements of Jews—though it must be admitted that in this connexion we should expect a name belonging to northern Egypt—and the description of the southern limit of Egypt as given in Ezek. xxx. 6 ('from Migdol to Syene') points in the same direction. It is not, of course, necessary to suppose that all these settlers were *Jews* in the strict sense of the term. Many of them may have migrated from Samaria. Life in Palestine must have been hard in the sixth century B. C., and there was every inducement to its inhabitants to migrate to a country which was less likely to be a perpetual battlefield. If we may suppose that the communities of Jews in Syene and other parts of Egypt were composed of immigrants from more than one district of Palestine, we can the more easily account for the fact that the language of the papyri is not Hebrew but Aramaic. It is probable that after the importation of colonists into the province of Samaria, Aramaic was there spoken almost to the same extent as Hebrew. Moreover, the words put into the mouth of Eliakim, Shebna, and Joah, though scarcely representing an actual speech in the reign of Hezekiah, not improbably reflect some incident in one of the later sieges of Jerusalem, and may at any rate be taken as evidence that in the last days of the kingdom of Judah many natives of Jerusalem understood Aramaic. Since the refugees who fled to Egypt from Judah belonged for the most part to the well-to-do classes—that is, to that section of the population which we may suppose to have been to a great extent bilingual—they would naturally adopt Aramaic as the medium of communication with the monoglot worshippers of Jehovah who had migrated to Egypt from Aramaic districts of Samaria. Certainly as early as the sixth century B. C. Aramaic was understood throughout Assyria and Babylonia proper, and was doubtless the official language of communication.

After the fall of Jerusalem in 586 Nebuchadnezzar set himself to subdue Tyre. The siege lasted from 585 to 572, and apparently even at the end of this long time the island city was still unsubdued. Ezekiel, who in 586 or 585 had expected the speedy ruin of Tyre (Ezek. xxvi), declared in 571 that since Nebuchadnezzar had had 'no wages, nor his army, from Tyre, for the service that he had served against it', he should have Egypt by way of compensation (chap. xxix. 17-20). A fragment of one of Nebuchadnezzar's inscriptions describes him as at war with Egypt in his thirty-seventh year (568-7 B.C.).

Nebuchadnezzar died in 561, and was succeeded by his son Amel-Marduk (Evil-merodach), who after a reign of two years was murdered by his brother-in-law Nergal-sharezer (Neriglissar). In 556 the latter was succeeded by his son Labashi-Marduk, whose nobles murdered him nine months later, and placed on the throne Nabunaid (Nabonidus), the son of Nabubalatshu-ikbi.

Meanwhile the Medes were rapidly increasing their power. Phraortes, their king, carried out successfully campaigns against Armenia and Cappadocia, and also waged war for five years against the kingdom of Lydia. A great battle against the Lydians having been interrupted by a total eclipse of the sun on May 28, 585 B.C., Nebuchadnezzar, who throughout his reign maintained friendly relations with the Medes, and the King of Cilicia acted as arbiters. Phraortes died in 585, and was succeeded by Astyages, whose empire included Anshan (an Elamite province with Susa for capital), of which Cyrus was a vassal prince. In 553, the third year of Nabonidus, a revolt took place in the Median empire against Astyages, whereupon the Persians under Cyrus revolted. About 551 Astyages was betrayed to Cyrus, who imprisoned him and sacked his capital Ecbatana. Cyrus thus succeeded to the throne of Media, and united the Medes and the Persians (i.e. Elam), or rather made the Persian portion of the Median empire, which had been subordinate, the more important.

Almost immediately after the overthrow of Astyages Cyrus was called to the north-west. Croesus, King of Lydia, having invaded Cappadocia, and thereby violated the treaty of 585, Cyrus advanced into Lydia, and took Sardis. Leaving his general Harpagus to complete the subjection of Lydia and the Ionian cities, Cyrus returned home, and spent the next few years in consolidating his rule in Persia. The conquest of Lydia had broken up a triple alliance between Lydia, Babylon, and Egypt, and in 539 Cyrus set himself to subdue the second of these powers. Nabonidus had alienated his Babylonian subjects, and his kingdom was weakened by internal dissensions. Belsharusur (Belshazzar), who was in command of the army, met Cyrus, but was defeated, and at the same time northern Babylonia revolted. Thereupon Sippar and Babylon opened their gates to Cyrus without resistance.

These events are apparently referred to in each of the two great divisions of the book of Isaiah, though the drastic revision to which the book has been subjected at a later date makes it difficult to determine the original form of the prophecies. Chap. xiii contains a prediction of Babylon's ruin at the hands of the Medes combined with a description of the Day of the Lord belonging to a later date, and chap. xiv contains a *māshāl* in which the poet gloats over the fall of the King of Babylon.

From which section of the Jewish people did these prophecies emanate? They contain several points of similarity with Jer. l, li, but chap. xiv in some respects also resembles Ezekiel. It is not necessary, however, to suppose any actual acquaintance on the part of the author with Ezekiel's prophecies. And since Ezekiel was of full age when he was taken into captivity, it may be that many of the phrases which he uses were already current in Judah in the days of Jehoiakim There is therefore no difficulty in supposing that these prophecies in their original form were composed in Palestine.

In Isa. xxi. 1–10 (though the passage has not come down to us in its original form) we have the words of a Palestinian prophet who is anxious for the fate of the Jews in Babylon when the city shall be given up to the soldiers of the conqueror. A barbarous foe, apparently identified in ver. 2 with Elam and Media, is advancing to plunder Babylon. The city is unprepared and is given up to feasting. Finally, the news comes of the fall of Babylon, but the prophet is unable to draw from it any consolation for his oppressed people.

The downfall of Babylon, which is the subject of the prophecies just mentioned, is dealt with again, and in some respects more definitely, in chaps. xl ff. Unfortunately the literary criticism of these chapters shows that they are extraordinarily complex, and it is no easy matter, if indeed it is possible, to sort out the various passages according to their several authors. Nowhere has the hand of the editor done such drastic work, and it is much easier to analyse than to reconstruct. Many indeed will be loth to believe that chapters of which the present effect is so beautiful can be a mere mosaic of fragments. The story of the Flood, however, in the book of Genesis is an illustration of the manner in which original documents could be rent asunder and recombined; and if such recombination is possible in narrative, how much more must it have been possible in passages containing but few definite historical allusions, and dwelling mainly on Israel's reasons for keeping faith in Jehovah. In Isa. xl–xlviii we read of the coming of Cyrus, of its effect on the world in general and on the Jews in particular, of the helplessness of the Babylonian idols, and of the greatness and wisdom of Jehovah; but these subjects are treated in fragments, undated and anonymous, which moreover are arranged in no discoverable order, and with them are combined other passages, apparently much later, which seem to have been primarily intended to encourage the Jewish Church in a struggle against the heathen.

It is obvious that in the case of mere fragments it is difficult with any certainty to fix either the exact date or place of their composition, and it is therefore not surprising that these chapters, made up as they are of fragments, have been variously ascribed both to Babylonian and to Palestinian prophets. Probably both views are to some extent true. That certain portions of these chapters are probably Palestinian will be shown later, but there is good reason for believing that at any rate some portions were composed in Babylonia.

Thus in the opening words of chap. xl, the prophet, whoever he may be, exhorts his hearers to comfort God's people, who, as the context shows, are the people of Jerusalem and, presumably, its neighbourhood. Since those who are bidden to give the comfort are obviously not the same as those who are comforted, it is reasonable to suppose that we have here an address to the Babylonian section of the Jewish Church— the section, that is to say, which stood in the closest relation with the coming of Cyrus—in which its members are bidden to comfort desolate Judah with the thought that at last her absent children will be restored to her. Associated with this prophecy we have (chap. xl. 9-11) a fragment of another similar prophecy, in which the Church in Babylon, personified as a woman, is exhorted to get up into a high mountain (perhaps having journeyed back by the road which Jehovah has ordered to be made ready for Himself and His people), and thence to proclaim to the cities of Judah the advent of Jehovah.

From the calm joy of xl. 1-11 as contrasted with (for example) xlvi. 1, 2, xlvii, xliv. 24-xlv. 7, in which victory over Babylon by force of arms seems to be contemplated, it may perhaps be inferred that it was composed when Babylon had opened its gates to Cyrus; possibly when the proclamation of Cyrus authorizing the restoration of the gods to their shrines and of captive populations to their homes had caused the Jews to hope that a similar clemency was to be extended to them.

Probably to this period should be assigned also the composition of the prophecy in Isa. lxi. 1 ff., which in its *original* connexion appears to have been a soliloquy put into the mouth of Cyrus.[1] Apart from

---

[1] The *original* reference to Cyrus is made probable by the fact that the speaker claims (lxi. 1) to have been anointed by Jehovah, and in xlv. 1 Cyrus is called Jehovah's anointed. The only other alternative, if the passage belongs

its historical meaning and its use by our Lord (St. Luke iv. 18, 19) the passage possesses an interest for us in the fact that it is apparently referred to by Ben Sira (Ecclus. xlviii. 24) as part of the book of Isaiah. Verse 7 also is perhaps quoted in Zech. ix. 12.

Other portions of these chapters are, however, composed in a different strain, and show that before the actual coming of Cyrus to Babylon there was a certain amount of anxiety among the Babylonian Jews as to their fate. This, as we have seen, is implied in chap. xxi, and it may perhaps be inferred also from a fragmentary verse (xlviii. 20), in which the Jews are exhorted to flee from Babylon, apparently in order that they may not be overwhelmed in its ruin. Whether this fragment is Babylonian or Palestinian it is impossible to say with certainty.[1] Similarly such passages as xli. 1–7, xlvi, xlvii, probably Babylonian in origin, appear to have been composed at a time when it was expected that Cyrus would treat Babylonia as the Chaldaeans had treated Judah. So also the section xliv. 24–xlv. 7, though in it Cyrus is hailed as conqueror and as the deliverer of the Jews, seems to anticipate a certain amount of opposition to him—opposition, however, which will be overborne by Jehovah.

Whether the hopes which were based on the coming of Cyrus found any realization is extremely doubtful. The discovery of the Cylinder inscription of Cyrus makes it clear that this king was by no means a monotheist, as he is represented in Ezra i, and there is no evidence that he gave permission to *all* the transported populations within his dominions to return to their original homes. He only mentions in this connexion Asshur and Susa, Agade, the land of Eshnunak (Umliash), Zamban, Mê-Turnu, and Dûr-ilu to the border of Qutû, the districts on the banks of the Tigris.[2] In fact, after the wholesale transportations which had been carried out by kings of Assyria and Babylonia within the two centuries preceding Cyrus's capture of Babylon, a general return of all the exiles in the empire to their several homes would have caused a ferment in Western Asia the end of which no one would have been able to foresee. It was Cyrus's policy to gain the goodwill of Assyria proper and Babylon, for he doubtless considered that, having gained this, he would be strong enough to suppress any risings in other

to this period, is to suppose that a *prophet* is the speaker; but it is difficult to believe that an *anointed* prophet would be anonymous. The anointing of a prophet is mentioned in 1 Kings xix. 16, and is apparently implied in Ps. cv. 15.

[1] This verse bears a strong resemblance to Zech. ii. 6, 7. Unfortunately, however, the latter passage is also fragmentary, and it is doubtful whether it is in its right context.

[2] See Pinches, *The Old Testament in the Light of the Historical Records of Assyria and Babylonia*, p. 422.

LECTURE II

portions of his dominions. The story of his giving back the Jews' sacred vessels is directly at variance with the statement of 2 Kings xxiv. 13—a statement which is not likely to have been invented by any one who had heard the story of Cyrus as given in Ezra i—and from Hag. ii. 6-8 it is a fair inference that in the second year of Darius there was little or no gold or silver in the Temple at Jerusalem. Moreover, Haggai and Zechariah consistently refer to the Persian empire in terms which show that they regard the King of Persia as the *oppressor*, not as the deliverer. It is also difficult to explain why, if free permission was given to the Jews in the first year of Cyrus (when the recollection of their Judaean homes must have been still fresh in the memories of many), such a vast number, and they, as the subsequent history shows, zealous for the faith of their fathers, preferred to remain behind in Babylonia. It is safe to conclude that in the book of Ezra we have the *inference* which a later Jew drew from the reference to Cyrus in the book of Isaiah, combined, perhaps, with some hazy knowledge of Cyrus's proclamation known to us from the Cylinder inscription. There is no evidence that the conquests of Cyrus made any immediate difference in the fortunes of the Jews.

Cyrus died about 529 B.C., and was succeeded by his son Cambyses, who in the fourth year of his reign invaded Egypt, which he entirely subdued. This invasion had momentous consequences for the Egyptian Jews. At Elephantine, where there was a large Jewish colony, a temple where sacrifices were offered to Jehovah was built at this time, and it seems to be suggested that it was the invasion of Cambyses which thwarted the opposition which the Egyptian priests had made to its building. In this way the worship of Jehovah, albeit worship of a kind which would hardly have been approved in Jerusalem, was being maintained in Egypt as well as in Babylonia.

Cambyses was succeeded in 522 B.C. by Darius I, who adopted a liberal conciliatory policy towards the subject states of his empire. To the Jews he showed his favour by appointing as governor of Judah a prince of the Judaean royal family named Zerubbabel.[1] This policy, it is true, may have been due more to a desire to keep the Jews loyal amid the wide-spread revolts which occurred at the beginning of the reign of Darius than from any particular goodwill towards them. It is remarkable that neither Haggai nor Zechariah shows any gratitude to Darius; while both prophets apparently hope for great things from the revolts in the east.

The appointment of Zerubbabel raised high hopes in the Jewish

[1] That it was Darius I, and not Darius II, who appointed Zerubbabel appears certain from Zech. i. 12.

community, which, however, were not to be realized. It is probable that Zerubbabel had inherited something of the old temper of the house of David, against which Isaiah and Jeremiah had contended in vain. It would seem that a scheme for fortifying Jerusalem, earnestly deprecated by the prophet Zechariah, aroused the suspicion of the Samaritans, who at this time acknowledged Jerusalem as the one legitimate sanctuary, and that they accused the governor of disloyalty to Darius. At any rate we hear no more of Zerubbabel, and the experiment of appointing a Jewish prince appears not to have been repeated.

To some extent, no doubt, the appointment of Zerubbabel must have brought the Babylonian Jews into closer touch with their Judaean brethren. It was not, however, till the latter half of the next century, under Nehemiah, that the unification of the two was accomplished, and then only at the cost of the Samaritan schism.

For some sixty years or so after the completion of the Temple the tension between Jews and Samaritans continually increased, culminating about 460–455 B.C. in an attack on Jerusalem by Samaritans, Ammonites, Moabites, and Edomites, who destroyed the wall which had apparently been just completed, and wreaked their vengeance on the city. For some few years Jerusalem lay at the mercy of its enemies; then came a sudden change in its fortunes. In 445 B.C. a Jew named Nehemiah was appointed by Artaxerxes governor of Judah, and about this time, though the exact year cannot be decided, there was an invasion of the countries bordering on the wilderness by Arabs, or at all events by people from the desert. Such invasions were not a new thing, for early in the sixth century Ezekiel had anticipated disaster to Ammon, Moab, and Edom from this direction; there is, however, no evidence that these nations suffered any serious calamity in this way till the days of Malachi, that is, about the time of Nehemiah.[1] Then indeed Edom, whose treacherous attack on them the Jews never forgave, was harried and left desolate, and it is probable that Moab suffered about the same time. To this period may be assigned the *original* composition of Isa. xv and xvi and perhaps xxi. 11 ff. For the foe who devastates Moab comes first upon Ar (by the Arnon), then upon Dibon (some four miles north of the Arnon), then upon Nebo in the north of Moab, and upon Medeba (some four or five miles south-east of Nebo). Thence the invaders

---

[1] It is not perhaps absolutely certain that the בְּנֵי קֶדֶם, 'children of the east,' are, strictly speaking, *Arabs*: they *may* be of Aramaean stock. At any rate they were Bedouin from the wilderness. The invaders of Edom, however, are not called בְּנֵי קֶדֶם and appear to have come from the south.

advance to Heshbon (five or six miles north-east of Nebo), thence to Nimrim in the north-west of Moab. Since the route of the enemy is from the south or south-east to the north or north-west, it is obvious that the Chaldaeans cannot be intended, but invaders from the wilderness. Chap. xvi, the text of which, however, is very mutilated, apparently belongs in its *original* form to the same date. It has, however, been re-edited at a much later date, when there again seemed to be a likelihood of the utter ruin of Moab (cf. ver. 13: 'This is the word that the Lord spake concerning Moab in time past. But now,' etc.).

For a century after the time when Nehemiah published the amalgamated law in Jerusalem, i.e. from 433–333 B.C., the history is nearly a blank. We are unable to fix precisely the date of the Samaritan schism, though, since it occurred during the governorship of Nehemiah, it was presumably within twenty years of the publication of the law.[1] The only other events, so far as the Jews are concerned, of which we have any knowledge are the appeal of the Elephantine Jews to Jerusalem about 411 B.C. for help to rebuild their temple, and the quarrel between the High Priest and his brother, which Bagoas, who had apparently succeeded Nehemiah as governor of Judah, made an excuse for levying a tax on the sacrifices at Jerusalem. The period generally appears to have been otherwise uneventful. The fact that Samaria had severed its connexion with Jerusalem, and that Nehemiah had quarrelled with the surrounding nations, makes it improbable that Judah was involved in the risings which took place in the days of Artaxerxes Ochus.

The reign of Artaxerxes Ochus, it is true, is believed by many to furnish a clue to the composition of at least many elements in Isa. xxiv–xxvii. Thus, to quote from a recent expositor, the Rev. G. H. Box[2] says: 'The most satisfactory solution, from every point of view, is that of Cheyne. This scholar assigns the Apocalypse to the latter years of the Persian period, when the Persian Empire was desolated by war, and was in the throes of dissolution (350–330 B.C.). During this gloomy time Judah must have suffered much from the collision of Persian and Egyptian forces. "The frequent passage of large Persian armies was itself a calamity for the Jews, and once, if not twice, the Jews appear to have been concerned in a revolt against Persia. Cruelly was their rebellion punished by the able but unscrupulous Artaxerxes Ochus" (Cheyne, *Introduction*, p. 155 f.). The gloomy description in

---

[1] Josephus, who brings the schism into connexion with the conquest of Palestine by Alexander the Great, is very hazy in his chronology of all this period.

[2] *The Book of Isaiah*, p. 113.

$27^{10, 11}$ refers to Jerusalem as it was soon after 347 B.C., after Artaxerxes, having reconquered Egypt, and destroyed Sidon, had wreaked his vengeance on the Jews for their share in the general rebellion. The songs of praise which the Jews *in far countries* raise in honour of Jahveh, referred to in 24^{14-15a}, were probably the result of Alexander the Great's victorious march through Asia Minor in 334 B.C. This will mark the *terminus ad quem* for the date of the composition of the Apocalypse proper. The date of the other pieces is probably somewhat later. Alexander's great victory at Issus has intervened. Cheyne, therefore, plausibly dates them circa 332 B.C.'[1]

But though there may have been some small risings among the Jews when Persian oppression was particularly galling, it must be confessed that the Jews' relations with their immediate neighbours from the time of Nehemiah onwards do not favour the supposition that the Jews took part in a *general* rising. It is noteworthy that those Psalms which have sometimes been assigned to this period[2] represent the surrounding nations (Ammonites, Moabites, etc.) as *hostile* to the Jews, not as allies, and the reference to Moab in Isaiah xxv. 10 ff. implies a similar point of view. Moreover, Judah need not necessarily have suffered from the passage of Persian or Egyptian armies, for the route of these would naturally be through the Philistine plain. Finally, the similarity of thought in these chapters to that found in late Psalms and in Zech. ix-xiv is a strong argument in favour of a later date.

In 333 B.C. Alexander the Great landed in the East and in the following year he had made himself master of Coele-Syria and Palestine. Notwithstanding the description of his kingdom in Daniel vii (which refers primarily to the extraordinary breaking up of old boundaries and kingdoms by Alexander), there is no reason to suppose that Judah suffered at his hands. Josephus, indeed, believed the contrary, but Josephus's chronology at this period is so chaotic, and his stories of the time just preceding the period of the Maccabees are so incredible, that he may, for our present purpose, be left out of account.

Although, as we have seen, portions of the remarkable collection of prophecies in chapters xxiv-xxvii are by some commentators assigned to this period, there are grave difficulties in the way of accepting this date for their composition. How, for example, could it have been said in the days of Alexander that Jehovah had extended all the boundaries of the land? (xxvi. 15). This collection contains a number of poetical fragments, but it is impossible to reduce it as a whole to any

[1] G. H. Box, *The Book of Isaiah*, p. 113.
[2] E. g. Pss. lx, lxxxiii.

poetical system. It seems to be the work of a later writer, or writers, who borrows freely, like the author of the book of Revelation, from the older Scriptures, the style of which he attempts to imitate. There are numerous parallels with the Psalms and also with the book of Daniel.

It is, however, not improbable that we have one passage composed at the time of Alexander's conquest of Palestine in the prophecy on Tyre (ch. xxiii). Unfortunately the text is mutilated in some places beyond restoration. It appears, however, that the poem was composed *after* a defeat of Tyre so crushing that the 'Tarshish ships' could no longer find there a harbour. The only time of which we have any information, when these words would appear to be justified, is that of Alexander the Great, who, having subdued Phoenicia with the exception of Tyre, constructed a causeway to the island-city through the sea, and took it in July 332 B.C. A difficulty in referring the prophecy to this date may, indeed, be found in the fact that Sidon is apparently associated with Tyre (verses 4, 12), whereas Sidon had opened its gates to Alexander. In some portions of the Old Testament, however, Sidon seems to be used as the name of the *country* of which Tyre was a chief city. Thus in 1 Kings v, Hiram is king of Tyre, but his subjects are Sidonians.

If this view is correct, ver. 1 *b* (which is much mutilated) is a reference to Alexander's coming from the land of Kittim (cf. Num. xxiv. 24, Dan. xi. 30, 1 Macc. i. 1). Then after a reference to the former trade of Tyre in verses 2, 3, the poet bids Sidon be ashamed, inasmuch as Tyre her greatest ornament is depopulated. The fall of Tyre is an ill omen for Egypt, of which, as a matter of fact, Alexander became master in 332 B.C.[1]

The later addition to the prophecy of Tyre (verses 17, 18), like the prophecy itself, is very obscure, and it is not easy to fix on a period of seventy years when Tyre was 'forgotten'. Indeed, after its ruin by Alexander, Tyre recovered its prosperity in a marvellous way. Although it was to some extent transformed into an Hellenic city, a large element, probably the majority of its population, was Phoenician. 'The coins of Tyre ... bear Phœnician legends alongside of Greek legends and the heads of the Macedonian rulers. As late as the Christian era there were many people in Tyre who did not even understand Greek.'[2]

[1] N.B. The use of the term בנעניה (ver. 8) favours a late origin. Similarly in ver. 11, כנען = Phoenicia, a usage quite different from that of Genesis. It is, however, impossible from the existing text to establish any theory with certainty, and the corruption is too deep to make emendation safe.

[2] Bevan, *The House of Seleucus*, vol. i, p. 229.

It is noteworthy that 'Tyre strikes coins of Ptolemy with an era dating from 275-274, that is, from about the time when hostilities' (as between Ptolemy and Antiochus I) 'were opened in Syria,'[1] and that in 202 B.C. Antiochus the Great became master of Tyre, where 'Seleucid coins were struck as early as 112 aer. Sel. = 201-200 B.C.'[2] Perhaps in this period of seventy-three or seventy-two years when Tyre was under the acknowledged dominion of the Ptolemies, we may see an explanation of the 'seventy years' of Isa. xxiii. 17, which is of course a round number. Though the condition of Judaea under the Ptolemies appears to have been far better than under Persian rule, the Jews had little love for their Egyptian masters, and when after the battle of the Panion in 198 B.C. Antiochus III took possession of Palestine, he was hailed by many in Judaea as a deliverer. Perhaps associations with the old Egyptian bondage in which their fathers had been made to serve with rigour had something to do with the Jewish dislike of Ptolemaic rule; but the transportation of a number of Jews to Egypt by Ptolemy Soter (if we may believe Josephus[3]) may well have embittered them. Moreover, the methods of men like the sons of Tobiah—though we need not assume the truth of all that Josephus relates—would not tend to make Egyptian government popular.

If then the Jews looked upon the time of Ptolemaic rule as one of oppression, it would not be unnatural for them to represent Tyre during the same period as 'forgotten'.[4] The conclusion of the appendix to the prophecy on Tyre—ver. 18, which is probably somewhat later than ver. 17—belongs to the same period as Ps. lxxxvii.

Though Jerusalem appears to have opened its gates to Alexander the Great, his coming had not less momentous consequences for the Jews than for Tyre. It had been the policy of Nehemiah—a policy abundantly justified by the event—to isolate the Jews from all the surrounding nations. For just one hundred years they had lived in a sort of Ghetto-like isolation, becoming every year more devoted to the Law, which was their peculiar glory, and more completely differentiated from the other nations of the earth.[5] Humanly speaking, had it not been for this century of isolation, Judaism must have been absorbed in Hellenism; for Nehemiah had found it no easy task to induce his people to keep the Law, and his work might have been

---

[1] Ib., p. 235.   [2] Ib., vol. ii, p. 32.   [3] See *Antiquities*, xii. 1.

[4] By 'the days of one king' we need not understand the life of one individual king. The expression here means 'the period of one domination'.

[5] The result of this isolation becomes apparent in the Macedonian period. While Samaritans, Edomites, and others gave up circumcision, and became more or less Hellenized, the Jews alone clung to their ancestral customs.

undone if Alexander had landed a century earlier. The period from 433 to 332 B.C. was the time of Israel's tutelage, when the nation was being prepared for the great work which God had chosen it to perform.

It is difficult for us adequately to realize the extraordinary change which the coming of Alexander brought about in the world of the Jews. At his death in 323 B.C. the old barriers had been broken down. East and west and north and south the way was open, and it was for the Jews to decide whether they would take advantage of it, or continue the old hemmed-in life, vainly looking for the restoration of the Hebrew monarchy, which, indeed, seemed as far off as ever. We may well imagine that the prospect of a freer mingling with the nations of the world after so long a period of isolation would be regarded by many religious Jews with dread. Doubtless there were not a few who argued that, if Nehemiah had laboured so earnestly to keep them from the contamination of Ashdod, he would have guarded them still more rigorously from the pollution of Macedonia. Happily, however, there were some in Judah who took a wider and a grander view. Imbued with the teaching of the prophet Malachi as well as the older prophets, they regarded Jehovah not as the God of Judah only, but also of the whole world. From the peculiar relation of Judah to Jehovah which their fathers had taught, and they themselves believed, they drew the lesson *Noblesse oblige*. Judah had been chosen and called by Jehovah not for Judah's sake alone, but for the sake of the whole world. In other words, Judah was to be to the world what the great prophets had been to Judah. It is to this period in all probability that the composition of the book of Jonah is to be assigned—that great allegory of Israel's mission, with its marvellous philanthropy and equally marvellous faith—a book which may probably be regarded as representing the dawning of Judah's consciousness of its missionary responsibilities. It is true that it is difficult, if not impossible, to fix precisely the date of an idea. That which strikes us to-day as having the force of novelty may have been familiar enough to our forebears. But if we may argue from such literature as we are able to date with tolerable certainty, we may reasonably maintain that there has not been preserved to us any passage of undoubtedly earlier date than the book of Jonah which embodies this missionary spirit in Judah.

But at this stage, before passing on to consider the remaining prophecies contained in the book of Isaiah, it will be well for us to attempt to gain some idea of the growth of the book. In the course of the present lecture we have observed that prophecies as late as, or later than, the time of Cyrus are not confined to the second great section (chaps. xl–lxvi), as might have been expected, but are found in the first section also; and therefore, since the well-marked division of the book into two main sections is not due to chronological arrangement, we must look to some other consideration for an explanation of it. From the reference to Isaiah in Ecclus. xlviii. 22 ff. it may be regarded as certain that in the time of Ben Sira (200-180 B. C.) there existed a book bearing the name of Isaiah which contained portions of each of the two great sections; and inasmuch as the prophecy which is now read, in lxi. 1 and which *in its original form* we have assigned to the time of Cyrus, appears to be actually quoted by Ben Sira, it is probable that this book contained also the other prophecies relating to the coming of Cyrus. We have also observed that some of the contents of this book appear to have originated in Palestine and others in Babylonia. Under what circumstances, therefore, were these heterogeneous elements combined into one book?

To such a question various answers may be given, and, though one may be more probable than another, there is little likelihood of our being able to decide the matter with absolute certainty. It is conceivable, perhaps, that the words of Isaiah the son of Amoz having been first committed to writing in Babylonia by the successors of Isaiah's original disciples, and there combined with a collection of prophecies by an unknown prophet of the Captivity, the document so composed was brought to Jerusalem in the time of Ezra, where it was combined with certain prophecies composed in Palestine, in order to bring the entire list of the prophetical books into harmony with a conventional number. If, however, this was the case, it is difficult to see why, for example, chaps. xiii, xiv, xxi. 1–10, which *ex hypothesi* would have been added to the book after it had been brought to Palestine, were not placed among the Cyrus prophecies.

Another more probable view is to suppose that the genuine words of Isaiah the son of Amoz were written down in Palestine at some time subsequent to Nebuchadnezzar's destruction of Jerusalem, and that there were afterwards appended to this book later predictions by Palestinian prophets relating to the downfall of Babylon because of the parallelism between these and Isaiah's great prediction of the downfall of Assyria. There may have been at the time of this earlier redaction some idea of assimilating the book of Isaiah to that of Jeremiah which contained a number of prophecies against the nations; and if so, after prophecies against Assyria and Babylon it would have seemed natural to add compositions directed against Moab, Edom, etc. When at the coming of Ezra the scriptures of the Babylonian Jews (including the book of Ezekiel) were brought to Palestine, the small anonymous collection of prophecies on the coming of Cyrus which had been composed in Babylonia was probably added to the Palestinian book of Isaiah, which contained predictions of the downfall of Babylon. Although there is no very obvious reason why the utterances of the Babylonian Jewish prophet should not have been preserved as a separate book, the words of Ben Sira may possibly furnish us with a clue. Since in his great list of the famous men of Israel, after mentioning by name Isaiah, Jeremiah, and Ezekiel, Ben Sira refers to the rest of the canonical prophets as 'the twelve Prophets', it is certainly not improbable that in his time the twelve minor Prophets already formed one book. The phrase 'the twelve Prophets' is remarkable, for in the absence of any distinguishing epithet applied to the prophets so enumerated one would naturally suppose the phrase to refer to *all* the canonical prophets; just as by 'the twelve Apostles' we understand *all* the members of the original Apostolic band. It must be confessed that the number *twelve* in this connexion is somewhat suspicious, and it is difficult to avoid the inference that its correspondence with the number of the tribes of Israel is not a mere coincidence. We have no means of deciding exactly at what date the first collection of prophetical books was made, but it is extremely probable that within a generation after the publication of the Law in 433 B.C. the Jewish Church at Jerusalem made a more or less authoritative collection of the Scriptures, which next to the Law it held in the highest reverence. Now the conception of Israel as a community consisting of twelve tribes is, as Kosters has pointed out,[1] peculiarly prominent in the account of the return from captivity under Ezra, and it is observable also in some late insertions in the book of Kings (e.g. 1 Kings xi. 29 ff., xviii. 31) which are probably later than the Samaritan schism. But if during the Persian period the prophets were reckoned as twelve in number, this enumeration must have included the greater prophets, for some at least of the minor prophets (e.g. Joel and Jonah, and perhaps Obadiah) are almost certainly later than the coming of Alexander. We cannot tell how the books were originally arranged, nor whether some now considered separate were originally reckoned together. It is certainly not impossible that Haggai and Zechariah originally formed one roll. On this supposition the greater prophets will have been separated from the rest when the recognition of later prophets (such as Joel and Jonah) as canonical made it impossible in any other way to retain the traditional number twelve.[2]

[1] *Encyclopaedia Biblica*, article *Ezra*, col. 1475.
[2] Similarly it is possible that the list of 'Judges' has been determined by a desire to make these twelve in number.

If then at the first formation of the canon of the Prophets, *twelve* was fixed as the conventional number, the primary aim of a Hebrew editor would be to arrange his documents in such a way as to produce twelve books; and if two of these documents, though of different origin, were parallel in their teaching, he would have little scruple in combining them into one book. On this hypothesis we can account for the combination of Palestinian and Babylonian documents.

Further, if the *nucleus* of the first section of the book of Isaiah is Palestinian, and the *nucleus* of the second section Babylonian, we are able to explain why the historical chapters were inserted between the two sections. There was also a certain suitability in making the prophecies of deliverance from Babylon follow the story of Isaiah's prediction of the captivity.

LECTURE III

MODIFICATION OF THE ENLARGED BOOK OF ISAIAH DURING THE MACCABAEAN PERIOD, AND ADDITION TO IT OF PROPHECIES RECENTLY COMPOSED

WE have seen that the Biblical account of the migration to Egypt from Palestine during the sixth century B.C. is confirmed by the papyri, from which we learn that in southern Egypt as early as 525 B.C. the immigrants had built a temple in which they offered sacrifices to Yahu (Jehovah). The present lecturer has argued elsewhere [1] from independent evidence that the book of Deuteronomy was not published in Jerusalem till after the murder of Gedaliah, and there is good reason for supposing that for some time neither the Jewish community in Babylon nor that in Egypt possessed any written law limiting sacrifice to one sanctuary. The reason that the Babylonian Jews did not, like their brethren in Egypt, build a temple to Jehovah in Babylon is probably to be found in the fact that they had in their midst the Zadokite priest Ezekiel, who had doubtless ministered in the Temple at Jerusalem, and who looked both for the rebuilding of that Temple and for the return from captivity. If we may suppose that the compact between southern Samaria (i.e. the district of which Bethel was the chief sanctuary) and Judah to make Jerusalem the one place of sacrifice for both districts [2] dates from a time subsequent to Nebuchadnezzar's destruction of Jerusalem, the law of Deuteronomy which embodies and extends this compact must be placed still later. It is practically certain from the book of Deuteronomy itself that the law of the One Sanctuary was only extended gradually over those districts which had originally belonged to the Kingdom of North Israel: it would seem that first southern Samaria accepted it; then northern Samaria (i.e. the district of which Shechem would be the chief sanctuary); then Galilee, to use the later name (i.e. the district north of, and perhaps including, the great plain of Megiddo); finally Gilead and Bashan beyond the Jordan. It is a fair inference from Joshua xxi. 32, which undoubtedly presupposes Deut. xix, that Kedesh in Naphtali and the surrounding district accepted the law of the One Sanctuary in the sixth century B.C. If then Naphtali (i.e. the district extending from near the later town of Tiberias up to the

---

[1] See 'The Date of Deuteronomy', *Journal of Theological Studies*, July, 1906.
[2] See 'The Origin of the Aaronite Priesthood', *Journal of Theological Studies*, January, 1905.

northern limit of Palestine) received the Deuteronomic law at this time, it is reasonable to suppose that Zebulun (i. e. the district to the south and south-west of Naphtali) did the same ; especially since of the two districts Naphtali had borne to a greater extent than Zebulun the brunt of Tiglath Pileser's invasion. The mention also of Golan in Bashan (Joshua xxi. 27) and Ramoth in Gilead (ib. 38) as cities of refuge proves that about the same time Bashan and Gilead accepted the law of the One Sanctuary. In addition to these, Bezer (two miles south-west of Dibon) in the tribe of Reuben, that is, in Moabite territory, is described as a city of refuge in Deut. iv. 43, Joshua xx. 8 ; but as it is not so described in the list of cities given in Joshua xxi, we may perhaps conclude that the Jewish population in Moab disappointed the hopes of the legislators (cf. Deut. xxxiii. 6).

But though the passages just referred to afford evidence that in the sixth century B. C. there existed in these outlying districts of the Holy Land an Israelitish (to use a comprehensive term) population more or less loyal to the Deuteronomic law, which would therefore be likely to accept in 433 the law published by Nehemiah, it would certainly be a great mistake to suppose that the population of these districts as a whole was Israelitish in the same degree as the population of Judaea or even of Samaria. Even apart from the colonists whom the kings of Assyria had introduced from various parts of their vast empire, Aramaeans from Coele-Syria and Damascus had for centuries been pouring into Bashan, Gilead, and Galilee. It must not be forgotten that Nehemiah sought to purify Judah from foreign influences not only by making Judah loyal to the Law, but also by expelling the foreigners— (cf. Neh. xiii). But though Nehemiah could carry his point with a high hand in Judah, where he was governor, he could not carry out so drastic a policy in Galilee and beyond the Jordan. The result was that in these districts the Jews, that is to say, those who accepted the Jewish law, were probably but a minority in a heathen population. It is likely that Zebulun and Naphtali might have been fittingly described as 'the circuit of the nations' (גְּלִיל הַגּוֹיִם).

What was the effect on these districts of the Samaritan schism ? Unfortunately of direct evidence there is none ; but it is probable that the schism affected *only the province of Samaria*, not the district to the north of it, nor yet the region beyond Jordan. Some slight indication of the religious condition of the non-Judaean portions of Palestine may perhaps be found in the account given in 2 Chron. xxx of the Passover in the reign of Hezekiah. The Chronicler's statements, where they are not borne out by other evidence, cannot always indeed be accepted as authoritative history for the period with which they ostensibly deal; for throughout his work the Chronicler ascribes to the past the conditions of his own time. It is, however, noteworthy that he represents as coming to Jerusalem to keep the Passover people from Asher (under which name he probably includes also Naphtali, which lay immediately to the east), Manasseh (i. e. perhaps, the part of Manasseh beyond Jordan, but possibly northern Samaria), and Zebulun; while later on in the same chapter (ver. 18) he speaks of some coming also from Ephraim (i.e. from Samaria). We may therefore conclude that the Chronicler, who, be it remembered, had a perfect horror of the Samaritan dissenters, whom he regarded as quite beyond the pale of Judaism, considered that many loyal Jews were to be found in the districts to the north and east of the province of Samaria, and—what is far more remarkable—some in Samaria itself.

This description of the Chronicler's, though we may hesitate to accept it as historically correct for the time of Hezekiah, probably gives a fairly accurate view of Palestine during the third century B. C. It is certainly likely that under Macedonian and Ptolemaic rule the Jews of the outlying districts were brought into closer touch with Jerusalem. For some time after the Samaritan schism, indeed, when the Jews of Judaea were at feud with all their immediate neighbours, it is not improbable that their co-religionists in Gilead, Bashan, and Galilee found it no easy matter to keep the feasts at Jerusalem: but during the first century and a half of Greek rule the influence of Judah and Jerusalem with the suzerain power appears to have increased, and it is probable that in the High-priesthood of Simon the son of Oniah, Jews from Galilee, Bashan, and Gilead could go up to the Temple at Jerusalem without let or hindrance.

We have no information as to the institution of synagogues, but we hear from Ezekiel that the elders of Israel were wont to assemble in his house, where he expounded to them the will of God; and as early as the time when the story of Elisha was written we hear of people betaking themselves to the prophets on holy days (new moons and sabbaths). In gatherings such as these we may well see the germ from which the synagogues developed; and indeed it is likely that we can actually point out the time when the development took place. In Nehemiah viii we have a description of the publication of the law (probably in the year 433 B.C.) to a large concourse of people in Jerusalem. Obviously, so complex a law could not have been learnt by the people on that one occasion. When those who had heard it read at Jerusalem returned to their homes, many a question must have cropped up which they would feel unable to answer without a careful exposition of the Law with reference to the present contingency. Considering the earnest efforts of Nehemiah and his supporters to make the Law a reality to the Jews, we cannot but conclude that provision was made for their *regular* instruction. Thus the institution of synagogues was the natural consequence of the work of Ezra and Nehemiah. The meetings at the houses of the prophets would become as a matter of course meetings for instruction in the Law.

But if in the meetings to hear the prophets we may see the germ from which the synagogues developed, we must recognize that with this development the old order changed, and gave place to something altogether new. The gift of prophecy did not necessarily carry with it a knowledge of the written *tôrā*; when, therefore, the written *tôrā* had been canonized, the prophet of necessity gave place to the scribe, that is to say, the *literatus*, the *doctor*, the man trained in the interpretation of that which had been made the authoritative rule of life. Not that the prophets as a class disappeared all at once. Zechariah xiii. 2-6 is evidence that an order of men calling themselves prophets, and wearing the old prophetic dress, existed as late as the second century B.C. There is no reason for regarding these men as mere imitators of an order that had long passed away. For even in the golden age of prophecy the words of the canonical prophets show conclusively that the *majority* of the prophets were unworthy of respect. It is sometimes objected by Jewish scholars that the denunciations of the Pharisees in the Gospels are altogether unjust. It must, however, be remembered that these denunciations are no sterner than those which we find the canonical prophets uttering against members of their own order. In fact, if we did not know that such men as, for example, Isaiah had accepted the title of *prophet*, we should be likely to conclude from a perusal of their words that *prophet* and *hypocrite* were synonymous terms. When therefore the oral teaching as to the will of Jehovah gave place to a written law, and the true prophet—the man who aimed at teaching his people faithfully the true will of Jehovah—gave place to the exponent of the written Scripture—in a word, when the place of the true prophets had been taken by the scribes, there remained as prophets only men of the type that Micah had held up to scorn. There were fools to be duped in the fifth, the fourth, the third, the second, centuries before Christ as there had been in the eighth, and as there are in this twentieth century of the Christian era. Men of the type that in the days of Micah had prophesied for a dinner[1] five hundred years after Micah's death still wore the hairy garment to deceive. Thus it came about that in the days in which the latest passages of the Old Testament were composed, those who had a great message to deliver to

[1] See Mic. iii.

their people no longer preached by word of mouth in the Temple courts or in the streets of Jerusalem. Had they done so, they could have collected an audience of the riff-raff of Jerusalem, but not those whose hearing they wanted to gain. Accordingly they put their message into the mouth of one of the saints of old—Job, Daniel, Enoch. The author of the book of Job is surely not less truly a prophet than Isaiah himself; but it was the institution of synagogues which indirectly decided the form in which his message was delivered.

We may, then, take it for granted that at the time when the Jews exchanged the rule of Darius for that of Alexander, synagogues were a recognized institution in all parts of Palestine, and that they existed also in Babylonia. Whether they existed in Egypt at this date is doubtful. In 411 B.C. the Jews of Upper Egypt apparently had not yet received the Law which had been published in Jerusalem in 433; and since the High Priest of Jerusalem had taken no notice of their communication to him, it is probable that they were regarded by their brethren in Judah with little favour. If the statement of Josephus [1] is to be believed that about 320 B.C. Ptolemy transferred a number of Jews from Jerusalem and Judaea, and also from Samaria, to Alexandria, and other places in Egypt, we may well believe that under their influence the Egyptian Jews would be brought to some extent into line with their Palestinian brethren. In any case, however, during the Ptolemaic rule, Judaean and Egyptian Jews would be brought into contact, and the Church of Jerusalem would naturally desire to win over the latter. No doubt it would require a good deal of persuasion to induce those who had been in the habit of sacrificing to Jehovah in Egypt to regard Jerusalem as the only legitimate place of sacrifice, and without a written law to appeal to, it would be impossible. Since Hebrew was not understood in Egypt, except perhaps by some of those who had been most recently transported thither, the original text of the Law was in Egypt a sealed book. The Egyptian Jews, therefore, could only be brought into line with their orthodox brethren by receiving the Law in their own vernacular. It is probable that to this exigency the real origin of the translation known as the Septuagint is due. It may well have been the case that, when the translation was made, it occasioned interest in circles other than the Jewish community; but we may feel pretty sure that the original motive, in making the translation, was not literary, not antiquarian, but a desire to supply the religious needs of Jews who in their ignorance of the Law were as sheep without a shepherd. It is certainly difficult to believe that the Jewish community in

[1] *Antiquities*, bk. xii, chap. i.

Egypt would have been content to accept as a Bible a translation which had originally been made only to give completeness to a library founded by a heathen king.

The Septuagint translation, that is, the Pentateuch, doubtless did for the Egyptian Jews what the publication of the Law by Ezra and Nehemiah had done for the Jews of Judah and Babylonia. In 433 B.C., by the amalgamation of the Babylonian and Palestinian Jewish law, two of the three separate sections of the Jews were brought into religious unity; by the translation of this amalgamated law into Greek this unity was extended to the third section also.

If this view of the origin of the Alexandrine version is correct, and it was only in the third century B.C. that the law of the One Sanctuary was at all generally recognized in Egypt, it is only reasonable to suppose that a considerable time would elapse before the Egyptian Jews as a whole accepted the Law with the whole-hearted loyalty of their brethren elsewhere. We can thus explain how it was that Oniah, when he built a temple at Leontopolis,[1] could find at least a good deal of support among Egyptian Jews; while from Zech. xiv. 18 we may perhaps infer that as late as the second century B.C. the attitude of Egyptian Jews towards Jerusalem still left something to be desired, though the threat may be aimed directly at the temple of Leontopolis.

It will thus be seen that in the third century B.C. the position of the Jewish Church in the world had enormously improved. True, Judah proper—i.e. that portion of the country about Jerusalem of which the population was predominantly Jewish—was a very small province, probably considerably smaller than Cambridgeshire; but its capital Jerusalem was regarded as the religious metropolis of Judaism by Jews in Gilead, Bashan, and Galilee, as well as in Babylonia and Egypt, in fact wherever Jews had been transported by their foreign rulers, or had settled in the way of business. Moreover, from Ben Sira's account of the great works which Simon carried out in Jerusalem (see Ecclus. l. 1-5) it is evident that at the end of the third century B.C. Jerusalem was no longer the poverty-stricken place which it had been in the days of the prophet Haggai, or even in the time of Nehemiah. Taxes, indeed, had to be paid to Egypt, and since the ways of oriental tax-gatherers are seldom all that could be wished, no doubt the lot of

---

[1] The schismatical action of Oniah is, on any view of the case, remarkable; but it may be that he interpreted the law of the One Sanctuary as meaning merely that there could only be one legitimate place of sacrifice in any portion of the world. He may have argued that, Jerusalem being in the hands of the heathen, another sanctuary must be built elsewhere.

the Judaean peasant was frequently anything but a happy one. On the other hand there were many wealthy and influential Jewish families. The revenues of the Temple were enormous, and supported a numerous priestly aristocracy of which the High Priest was the head. The High Priest appears to have been the virtual, if not the actual, ruler of Judah proper.

Of this small Jewish province Jerusalem was incomparably the most important place. Within the boundaries of the district occupied mainly by Jews there were few other towns of any importance, so that some two hundred years before Christ the names Judah and Jerusalem virtually denoted country people and townspeople respectively. And here we have a clue to the interpretation of the history of the great struggle between Judaism and Hellenism. It had been the policy of Alexander and his successors to found throughout the empire nominally free cities after the Greek model. It was in the *cities* of Syria and Palestine, therefore, that the results of the Macedonian conquest were most evident. In the cities Greek was spoken by the educated classes, and Greek ideas were everywhere forcing a way. In the country, on the other hand, Greek influence was comparatively little felt. The Judaean peasant who took the produce of his land to Jerusalem for sale might hear Greek spoken, and see people wearing a strange and new-fangled dress, but his own thought and conduct were no more affected by what he heard and saw than the thought and conduct of the country people who come in every Saturday to the Cambridge market is directly affected by the University under whose shadow they sell their butter and chickens and vegetables.

Under such circumstances it is not surprising that there should have been a gradually widening rift between Jerusalem and the country districts of Judah. Not, of course, that every one in Jerusalem was equally bitten by Hellenism and every one in the country equally opposed to it; only that the dominant influence in Jerusalem was not the same as the dominant influence in Judah.

Down to the days of Ben Sira, the High Priest appears to have kept in check the more ardent Hellenizers in Israel. Hellenism, it is true, had affected orthodox Judaism, but it had acted rather as a stimulus to thought, which remained truly Jewish,[1] than as changing the character of that thought.

The members of the conservative Jewish party, which, as we have

---

[1] Thus the development of the 'wisdom' literature which falls in this period was no doubt stimulated by the presence of Greek philosophy, but it cannot be too emphatically stated that the wisdom is *Hebrew* wisdom. Nowhere in the Old Testament, unless it is in Ecclesiastes, are there any traces of Greek *thought*.

seen, was most strongly represented in the country districts, came to be called Ḥasîdîm (A.V. *Assideans*, R.V. Hasidaeans).[1] We do not know the origin of the name; that is to say, whether those who were so called had originally applied the name to themselves, or whether it was a nickname bestowed on them by their opponents, and ultimately accepted by them as an honourable title. In any case it denotes those who specially insisted on the quality of *ḥesed*, piety.

It may be that the delight which the Jews felt at being freed from Ptolemaic rule in 198 B.C. disposed them to look more favourably on the Seleucid king, Antiochus III, than they had ever looked on the Ptolemies; and if so, it was but natural that they should be more open to Macedonian influences coming through Antioch than to those which had come to them through Egypt. Certainly from about this time leaven of Hellenism was working rapidly in Jerusalem and among the upper classes of Judah. One sign of the passing away of the old order is to be found in the Greek names which we now find borne by Jews. Thus in the reign of Seleucus IV (187–176 B.C.) we find a Jew whose father bears the Hebrew name Tobijah with the Greek name Hyrcanus,[2] and Jeshua, the younger son of Simon the Just, takes the name of Jason.[3]

Oniah the son of Simon, whom we find High Priest in the reign of Seleucus IV, appears to have had little or no sympathy with the Hellenizing movement, and accordingly, though he was reverenced by the Ḥasîdîm, i. e. the poorer members of the community, he found no support among the influential Jewish families. Even his own brother Jeshua or Jason was an ardent Hellenizer.

The beginning of trouble, according to the account given in 2 Maccabees, was a quarrel between Oniah and a certain Benjamite aristocrat named Simon; in consequence of which the latter slandered the High Priest to Seleucus, until Oniah, finding his position in Jerusalem precarious, left the Holy City in order to represent his case to Seleucus at Antioch.[4]

---

[1] The spelling of the Greek Ἀσιδαῖοι suggests that the word was current in Egypt in an Aramaic form, viz. חֲסִידָא pl. חֲסִידַיָּא.

[2] 2 Macc. iii. 11.   [3] Josephus, *Antiquities*, bk. XII, chap. v, § 1.

[4] Since it is clear that the good shepherd of Zech. xi who feeds the flock of slaughter (i. e. the Jewish people) for the sheep merchants (i. e. the Seleucid kings, who were ready to sell to the highest bidder the High-priesthood and with it the Jewish people) is the chief *Jewish* ruler, it seems scarcely possible that any one but Oniah can be intended. Unfortunately the passage has not come down to us entire: there is a *hiatus* between ver. 7 and ver. 8, and again one between ver. 8 a and ver. 8 b. Verse 9 probably refers to Oniah's determination to leave Jerusalem, and ver. 12 to an appeal made by him to his flock for funds to enable

So long as the High Priest, the head of the Jewish community, was himself loyal to the law of his fathers, and remained to protect his people, the Hellenizers, however much they might despise the Hasîdîm, could not openly persecute them; but when the good shepherd was taken away, evil days came upon the flock of the Lord. In 176 B.C. Seleucus IV was murdered in a conspiracy formed against him by his ambitious minister Heliodorus. His elder son, Demetrius, who at the time of his father's murder was about nine years old, was then in Rome, whither he had been sent as a hostage. Another son, an infant, was probably proclaimed king by Heliodorus.[1] Thereupon Antiochus, the brother of the late king, who was living at Athens, crossed over into Asia Minor, and with the help of Eumenes of Pergamos declared himself king of Syria. It was not long before he succeeded in winning over the kingdom of his brother. The infant son of Seleucus he contrived to have assassinated. The true heir to the throne, however, was in Rome, safe from Antiochus's clutches.

It was the policy of Antiochus IV, or, to give him the name by which he is more commonly known, Antiochus Epiphanes, to weld together his heterogeneous empire, consisting of 'all peoples, nations, and languages', by encouraging everywhere the adoption of Hellenism. It was no wonder therefore that under such a ruler the Hellenizing party at Jerusalem began to assert themselves. At the beginning of the reign of Antiochus (i.e. in 175 B.C.) Jason, the brother of Oniah, by the promise of a large sum of money induced the King to appoint him High Priest in place of his brother, who still remained at Antioch, at the same time applying for permission to remodel Jerusalem as a Greek city. A gymnasium was built there, and the young Jewish aristocrats adopted Greek dress.

It is noteworthy that Jason and his faction, however far they may have been from showing themselves blameless as touching the righteousness which is in the Law, appear to have been guilty of no definite act of apostasy. It is indeed related by the author of 2 Maccabees that 'the envoys of Jason to the games at Tyre were unwilling to contribute to the sacrifice to Heracles, and obtained leave to divert the money they carried to a secular purpose.'[2] But though neither the gymnasium nor Greek dress in themselves constituted apostasy,

---

him to defend himself at Antioch. Oniah must have known that without money his case was hopeless; but the richer people in Jerusalem had little sympathy for him, and the Hasidim had little money to bestow. The sum subscribed was so small—it is compared to the amount specified by the Law (Exod. xxi. 32) as compensation for injury done to a slave—that Oniah indignantly repudiated it.

[1] See Bevan, *House of Seleucus*, vol. ii, p. 126.   [2] Ibid., p. 170.

they exposed their votaries to temptation to apostasy—temptation to which, as a matter of fact, many Jews yielded.[1] It must not be forgotten that, save for the fact that his brother Oniah was still living, Jason was the legitimate High Priest.

Jason did not long retain the High-priesthood which he had obtained so unscrupulously. He was destined soon to find out that the tools which he had used against his brother could be used against himself. Within three years, Menelaus, a Benjamite, the brother of the Simon who had intrigued against Oniah, began to intrigue against Jason. Antiochus was in need of money, and Menelaus, by promising to pay to him a larger sum than Jason had paid, found little difficulty in getting himself appointed High Priest. The garrison which Antiochus had in the citadel of Jerusalem made resistance on the part of Jason hopeless. He was compelled to flee to the country east of the Jordan, and Menelaus reigned in his stead. As a Benjamite Menelaus was, of course, quite ineligible for the High-priesthood, and no doubt many whose sympathies were on the whole with the Hellenizers were not prepared for so violent a breach of the Jewish law. Fearing probably that his position would be insecure while Oniah lived, Menelaus bribed Andronicus, whom Antiochus had left in charge of affairs at Antioch, to murder him. The conduct of Menelaus in the position which he had usurped was so outrageous, that in all probability after the death of Oniah the Ḥasîdim as well as the more moderate of the Hellenizers gave their sympathy to Jason. Inasmuch, however, as Menelaus had been appointed by Antiochus, it was easy to represent any opposition to him as disloyalty to the King. For some time, however, there was no open revolt.

In 170-169 B.C. war broke out between Antiochus and his young nephew, Ptolemy Philometor, King of Egypt. The regents Eulaeus and Lenaeus, in whose hands was the government, were confident of recovering Coele-Syria for Egypt. Antiochus, however, met the Egyptian army near Pelusium, and utterly defeated it, and shortly afterwards the young King Ptolemy, who had attempted to escape, was captured by Syrians, and fell into the hands of Antiochus. Thereupon the people of Alexandria made king the youngest brother of Ptolemy Philometor with the surname Euergetes. At the beginning of the war, Antiochus had not been the aggressor, but the turn of events had now given him a pretext for the invasion of Egypt. He represented himself as the champion of the rightful king, Ptolemy Philometor, against his usurping brother, and as such found a con-

---

[1] See 1 Macc. i. 15

siderable amount of support among the Egyptians. He seized Pelusium, and was soon master of all lower Egypt except Alexandria. 'The seat of the rival government for which Ptolemy Philometor was to serve as figure-head'[1] was fixed at Memphis. In a short time Antiochus had begun the siege of Alexandria, and a general panic prevailed.

It is in all probability to this period that we should assign the prophecy in Isa. xix, 1-15. It must be remembered that the Jews had no love for the Ptolemaic rule, and that they had welcomed Antiochus III as a deliverer. Antiochus Epiphanes had as yet shed no blood in Jerusalem. He was not held responsible for the murder of Oniah;[2] and if he had favoured the Hellenizers, and put into the High-priesthood a man unqualified for the office, there was no reason to suppose that a Ptolemy would in such respects prove a better ruler, especially since the Sons of Tobiah, the chief supporters of Menelaus, had in the old days been supporters of Ptolemaic rule. The dread of passing again under the Egyptian yoke must have been dissipated by the news of Antiochus's victory over the Egyptian army, and it seemed as though Antiochus were the scourge in the hand of the Lord to chastise the boastful Egyptian nation. We have a reference to the suddenness of Antiochus's attack on Egypt, and the panic caused by it, in the words of ver. 1: 'Behold, Jehovah rideth upon a swift cloud, and cometh to Egypt; and the idols of Egypt will be moved at his presence, and the heart of Egypt will melt in the midst of it.' The conditions of things in Egypt after Antiochus's seizure of Pelusium, when a state of civil war prevailed (Antiochus, who represented Ptolemy Philometor, being opposed to Alexandria, which had made Ptolemy Euergetes king), is clearly indicated in ver. 2: 'And I will incite Egypt against Egypt, and they will fight one against his brother, and one against his friend; city against city, kingdom against kingdom.' In the 'hard master' (אֲדֹנִים קָשֶׁה) and the 'stern king' (מֶלֶךְ עַז) into whose hand Egypt is to be given, there is a reference to Antiochus Epiphanes, who is described in the book of Daniel (chap. viii, 23) as 'stern-faced' (עַז פָּנִים), and in the Sibylline Oracles (iii. 389, 390) as ἀνὴρ πορφυρέην λώπην ἐπιειμένος ὤμοις, ἄγριος, ἀλλοδίκης, φλογόεις.[3] In ver. 13 we may see a reference to Pelusium, for Zoan (i.e. Tanis, eight miles north-west of Pelusium) is used (e.g. Ps. lxxviii. 12, 43) as the name of the *district* in which Pelusium stood; and Noph is, of course, Memphis, where Antiochus fixed his government. The Egyptians had good cause to complain of their

---

[1] *House of Seleucus*, vol. ii, p. 137.   [2] 2 Macc. iv. 37.
[3] Quoted by Driver, *Daniel*, Camb. Bible for Schools, p. 98.

leaders who had brought matters to such a pass: 'those who were the corner-stones of the tribes' of Egypt had 'misled' their people.[1]

For some unexplained reason Antiochus suddenly raised the siege of Alexandria, and returned to Syria, retaining however a garrison in Pelusium, and leaving Ptolemy Philometor reigning at Memphis in opposition to his brother Ptolemy Euergetes, at Alexandria. But his plans were upset by a reconciliation between the brothers, who, it was arranged, were to reign as joint-kings. Antiochus had therefore no excuse for the continued occupation of Egypt; nevertheless he was determined not to be baulked in his schemes. In the spring of 168 B.C. he again invaded Egypt, but when he seemed to hold the country almost in the hollow of his hand, he was suddenly compelled by the intervention of Rome to evacuate it.

Meanwhile the storm which the writer of Isaiah xix. 1-15 had expected to devastate Egypt broke upon Jerusalem. During Antiochus's campaign of 170-169[2] a false report had reached Jason in the Ammonite country that the king was dead. Thereupon, having by some means collected a band of one thousand men, Jason suddenly attacked and took Jerusalem. Menelaus was compelled to take refuge in the citadel, which was held by a garrison of Syrian troops. A large number of his supporters, i.e. the party friendly to the Syrian government, were massacred by Jason. During the struggle between the rival factions in Jerusalem a certain amount of injury appears to have been done to the Temple, of which one, or more, of the gatehouses was burnt.[3] This attack on the nominee of Antiochus was not unnaturally

[1] The apocalyptic character of this prophecy, with its quotations from, and implied references to, older passages of Scripture, is in harmony with a late date. The figure of the drying up of the river (ver. 5) is employed to denote the ruin of the nation, since the life of Egypt depended upon the Nile. Other prophets (cf. xlii. 15; l. 2) state generally Jehovah's power to dry up the sea. The thought here is perhaps derived from the curse on the Nile in Exod. vii. 14-21.

The text of this prophecy has certainly suffered to some extent. The form of verses 11 b, 12 a suggests that Pharaoh is directly addressed, and that the passage should run: 'How sayest thou, O Pharaoh, I am the son of the wise, the son of ancient kings?' (i.e. אֵיךְ תֹּאמַר פַּרְעֹה).

The use of the name *Pharaoh* is no argument against the date here assigned to this prophecy, for 'in old Coptic (of the second century A.D.) the descendant of Pr'-o is simply ΠΕΡΟ "the king"' (Hastings' *Dictionary of the Bible*, art. *Pharaoh*, p. 819.)

Verses 16, 17 would seem to be an appendix to the prophecy though of much the same date. The meaning is that so terribly will Jehovah have avenged the wrong done by Egypt to the land of Judah, that to the Egyptians the very name of Judah will be ominous of evil.

[2] See *House of Seleucus*, vol. ii, p. 297, Appendix G.

[3] Cf. 1 Macc. iv. 38; 2 Macc. i. 8, viii. 33.

regarded by the king as a revolt against his rule, and on his return from Egypt he marched to Jerusalem to crush the rebellion. Jason had already fled to the Ammonite territory, but the Holy City bore all the brunt of Antiochus's wrath. For three days there was an indiscriminate massacre by the Syrian soldiery. Antiochus, guided by Menelaus, entered the Temple, which he stripped of its treasures.

After the collapse of his plans in Egypt, Antiochus again turned his attention to Jerusalem. The story of what followed has been so admirably told by Mr. E. R. Bevan that it cannot be given better than in his own words.[1] 'Since Antiochus could no longer after 168 protect the Cœle-Syrian province by holding any Egyptian territory, its internal consolidation became imperative in the first degree. The weak spot was Jerusalem. What the Seleucid court believed it saw there was a loyal party, readily accepting the genial culture which was to harmonize the kingdom, on the one hand, and on the other a people perversely and dangerously solitary, resisting all efforts to amalgamate them with the general system, and only waiting the appearance of a foreign invader to rebel. And on what ground did this people maintain its obstinate isolation? On the ground of an unlovely barbarian superstition. Very well: the religion of Jehovah must be abolished. The Hellenization of Jerusalem must be made perfect. If part of the population took up an attitude of irreconcilable obstruction, they must be exterminated and their place filled by Greek colonists.

'Apollonius, the commander of the Mysian mercenaries, was charged with the first step of effecting a strong military occupation of Jerusalem. His errand was concealed; he went with a considerable force, ostensibly in connexion with the tribute from southern Syria, and seized Jerusalem by a *coup de main*. A fresh massacre, directed probably by Menelaus and his adherents, cleared Jerusalem of the obnoxious element. A new fortress of great strength was built on Mount Zion, and a body of royal troops, "Macedonians," established in it to dominate the city.

'But now came the second part of the process, the extinguishing of the Jewish religion. It was simple enough in Jerusalem itself. Jehovah was identified with Zeus Olympius, and Zeus Olympius, it would appear, with Antiochus. The ritual was altered in such a way as to make the breach with Judaism most absolute. A Greek altar— the "Abomination of Desolation"[2]—was erected upon the old Jewish altar in the Temple court, and swine sacrificed upon it. The High-priest partook of the new sacrificial feasts, of the "broth of abominable

---

[1] *House of Seleucus*, vol. ii, p. 172 ff.   [2] 1 Macc. i. 54.

things ". To partake was made the test of loyalty to the King. The day of the King's birth was monthly celebrated with Greek rites. A Dionysiac festival was introduced, when the population of Jerusalem went in procession, crowned with ivy. That everything might conform to the purest Hellenic type, the framing of the new institutions was entrusted to one of the King's friends from Athens.[1]

'At the same time that the transformation was accomplished in Jerusalem, the other temple built to Jehovah in Shechem, the religious centre of the Samaritans, was constituted a temple of Zeus Xenios.

'To purge Jerusalem of all trace of Judaism was comparatively easy; it was another matter to master the country. In the country villages and smaller towns of Judæa the royal officers met with instances of extreme resistance. Their instructions were to compel the population to break with the old religion by taking part in the ceremonies of Hellenic worship, especially in eating the flesh of sacrificed swine, and to punish even with death mothers who circumcised their children. The books of which the Jews made so much were destroyed if found, or disfigured by mocking scribbles, or defiled with unholy broth.'

These events are pretty clearly referred to in more than one passage of the book of Isaiah. Thus the section lvi. 9–lvii. 13, which is to a great extent an imitation of older prophecy,[2] begins with a sarcastic invitation to wild beasts to come and devour the flock of the Lord, inasmuch as those who should act the part of sheep-dogs and shepherds care only for their own ease and gain.[3] And in consequence the righteous man perishes, and none interposes to save him, and men of piety (Heb. *ḥesed*, i. e. the Ḥasîdîm) are taken away. Jerusalem has forsaken her true husband Jehovah, and has joined herself to a foreign god. The offspring of this guilty union,[4] i. e. the Hellenizing Jews, mock the Ḥasîdîm and ridicule them.[5] A high and lofty mountain,

---

[1] Cf. 2 Macc. vi. 1.

[2] It cannot be too strongly insisted upon that *early phrases* are no evidence that the passage in which they occur was composed at an early date, as is proved by a study of the Apocalypse of S. John, which abounds in quotations from, and imitations of, the Old Testament.

[3] For this denunciation of the shepherds compare Zech. xi. 15-17, which was certainly composed about this time, and probably refers to Menelaus.

[4] Compare the use of the term 'bastard' (מַמְזֵר) in the nearly contemporary passage Zech. ix. 6, which refers to the mixed population, half Philistine, half Greek, of the Philistine cities.

[5] Verse 5 is apparently inserted here by an editor from another, probably much older, prophecy. That it was not originally part of its present context is proved by the fact that it is written in a different rhythm, and uses the word יְלָדִים in a different sense from that which it bears in ver. 4.

LECTURE III 57

i. e. Jerusalem, is the scene of this idolatrous worship.[1] Though the doors and doorposts are inscribed with Jehovah's name (cf. Deut. vi. 9), idolatrous symbols are in the background. Jerusalem has striven to make herself attractive to the King (i. e. Antiochus Epiphanes) like a woman who strives to increase her charms with choice scents,[2] and has sent embassies to heathen cities far off.[3] Are the Jerusalem people afraid of Antiochus Epiphanes, that they thus dissemble their religion and profess to be Greek ?

Again in chapter lxv we have a vehement denunciation of idolatrous practices, most, if not all, of which are to be found on Greek soil. Jehovah complains that He has revealed Himself in vain to people who seek Him not; people who sacrifice in gardens, and burn incense upon bricks; who sit among the graves, and lodge in the secret places; who eat swine's flesh, and in whose vessels is broth of abominable things; who say that they are holy, and must not be touched by those who are not purified like themselves.[4] Now we know that there was at Athens a cult of Aphrodite in the Gardens (Ἀφροδίτη ἐν κήποις), who was worshipped in the north-west of the Acropolis[5]; and that in the enclosure sacred to this goddess certain mysteries were performed. It is reasonable to see in the gardens mentioned in this chapter and also in lxvi. 17, i. 29 a reference to this cult.

The burning of incense or other sacrifice on *bricks* is rather difficult to explain. A movable incense altar of terra cotta was found at Tell Ta'annek (the Taanach of the Bible) a description of which has been given by Professor Driver in his *Schweich Lectures, 1908*, pp. 84, 85; but it is scarcely possible that the word לְבֵנָה, which means properly *brick* or *tile*, could be used to mean earthenware generally. But in the Heroum of Olympia a small quadrangular altar was found, which

---

[1] The language of much of this passage seems to be an imitation of Ezek. xvi.
[2] The text here is not above suspicion, but this seems to be the meaning.
[3] Compare 2 Macc. iv. 18-20.
[4] Instead of קְדַשְׁתִּיךָ, which is translated—though it cannot possibly bear such a meaning—'I am holier than thou,' we must read קָדַשְׁתִּי 'I am holy'. The final *kaph* of קדשתיך is probably only the first letter of the word כִּי ('for'), with which the next verse should begin. The suggestion that only the pointing of the Masoretic text should be changed, so as to read the *Pi'el* for the *Kal*, and that the clause should be translated, ' for I should sanctify thee,' though made by one of the greatest scholars of the last century, Robertson Smith, cannot be accepted. The sense which he proposed to give to the clause would be expressed in Hebrew by פֶּן־אֲקַדֶּשְׁךָ. On the purificatory rites performed in connexion with the mysteries see Harrison, *Prolegomena to the Study of Greek Religion*, pp. 151 ff.
[5] See Frazer, *Pausanias' Description of Greece*, vol. i, pp. 26, 40, vol. ii, p. 344 f.; Harrison, *Prolegomena to the Study of Greek Religion*, p. 132.

Professor J. G. Frazer describes as follows :[1] 'It is formed simply of hard earth mixed with ashes and charcoal, but is covered on the top with a broad flat brick. The three visible sides' (the fourth being close to the wall) 'were coated with plaster and painted. The altar rests on the ground without any steps; its dimensions are as follows: length ·54 metre, breadth ·38 metre, height ·37 metre. That burnt sacrifices were offered on the altar is clear from the marks of fire on its top, as well as from the ashes and charcoal that were found. On both sides were observed the traces of libations that had flowed down here. The plaster on the front and sides had plainly been often renewed, and as it exhibited traces of paintings and letters, the German excavators had it peeled carefully off on the front. Thus they discovered no less than twelve successive coats of plaster. Almost every coat had a leafy branch or two painted on it, the stalks being coloured brown and the leaves green. . . . Moreover, on each coat was painted in violet letters the word ΗΡΩΟΡ or ΗΡΩΟΣ ("of the hero") or ΗΡΩΩΝ ("of the heroes"). Thus we learn that the altar was sacred to a hero or heroes.[2]'

The interest of the Heroum for our purpose lies in the fact that it seems to have served as the model for the Philippeum, which was begun by Philip of Macedon in 338 B.C., and completed by Alexander the Great.[3] Although no traces of any altar, brick or otherwise, have been found in this building, the builders appear to have had some special reason for preferring *brick* to stone. Pausanias indeed states that it was built of baked bricks, but the present lecturer is informed by his friend and colleague Mr. A. B. Cook, who first called his attention to the brick altar in the Heroum, that it was in reality built of stone which was *painted to represent brick*. It must not be forgotten that Antiochus Epiphanes before his accession had been living at Athens, and 'had not only become an Athenian citizen, but had even been elected to the chief magistracy (that of στρατηγὸς ἐπὶ τὰ ὅπλα)'.[4] Further, in order 'that everything might conform to the purest Hellenic type, the framing of the new institutions was entrusted to one of the king's friends from Athens'.[5] Here, therefore, although more light on the subject is desiderated, we have an illustration of the ritual which so horrified the Ḥasîdîm, viz. the burning of sacrifice on altars or hearths of brick, in defiance of the law (Exod. xx. 25) which requires unhewn stone.

---

[1] *Pausanias' Description of Greece*, vol. iii, p. 579.
[2] See also *Olympia, Die Ergebnisse*, vol. ii.
[3] Frazer, *op. cit.*, p. 622 seq.   [4] Bevan, *House of Seleucus*, vol. ii, p. 126.
[5] Bevan, *op. cit.*, p. 173.

LECTURE III

The exact nature of the heathenish practices next mentioned is not quite clear. It has been held that the special object of those 'who sit in the graves and pass the night in the secret places' was to get inspired dreams (by *incubatio*) or, possibly, necromantic oracles.[1] The context, however, seems to imply not mere ordinary necromancy such as is prohibited in Deut. xviii. 11, but a *mystery* which would be an integral part of some heathenish worship.

On the eating of swine's flesh (lxv. 4) there is no need to dwell; for the books of Maccabees distinctly state that the Jews were required to partake of such sacrifices, and it is well known that swine were sacrificed by the Greeks.[2]

Further on in the same chapter we find another reference to foreign superstitions which points in the same direction. 'Ye that forsake the Lord,' writes the prophet, 'that forget my holy mountain, that prepare a table for Fortune (*Gad*, גד), and that fill up mingled wine unto Destiny (*Měnî*, מני).' By forgetfulness of Jehovah's holy mountain we are probably to understand the ignoring of the Temple's claim to be the *only* sanctuary by the erection of altars elsewhere.[3] Now 'Gad is the name of an old Semitic god of fortune, mentioned particularly in Aramaic inscriptions from Hauran and Palmyra,'[4] who seems to have been worshipped in Palestine in early times (cf. Joshua xi. 17, xii. 7, xiii. 5, xv. 37); and accordingly it has been supposed that we have here a reference to some Aramaean cult. If this were the case, however, we should expect *Měnî* mentioned in the parallel clause to be likewise the name of a Semitic deity, and of this there is no evidence. It seems, therefore, more probable that we should regard both *Gad* and *Měnî* as *translations*. Certainly, by those who did not speak Greek, *Baal* was used as the equivalent of *Zeus*,[5] and there is therefore no difficulty in supposing that Semitic equivalents were found for the names of other Greek divinities. If then *Gad* be regarded as a translation of a Greek name, there can be little difficulty in identifying the original. The cult of Τύχη, *Fortune*, was introduced into Syria in the Macedonian period. Antioch had a temple of Τύχη, which possessed a representation of the goddess seated upon a rock with the river Orontes at her feet.[6] We have evidence also of the existence of the same cult much nearer to Jerusalem, e.g. in Philistia, where the Hellenizing policy of Antiochus

---
[1] Cheyne, *Introduction to the Book of Isaiah*, p. 366.
[2] See Harrison, *Prolegomena*, p. 153; Frazer, *Pausanias*, vol. iii, p. 593.
[3] See 1 Macc. i. 54.   [4] Driver, *The Book of Genesis*, p. 274.
[5] A. A. Bevan, *The Book of Daniel*, p. 193.
[6] See Bevan, *House of Seleucus*, vol. i, p. 213; vol. ii, plate iv. 11.

Epiphanes seems to have met with little or no opposition.[1] Thus Gaza possessed a temple of Τύχη, and the name occurs also on coins of Ashkelon.[2]

In the allusion to the spreading of a table and the filling up of mixed wine Dr. Skinner sees a reference to the '*lectisternia*, well known throughout the ancient world, in which a table was spread furnished with meats and drinks, as a meal for the gods'.[3] It is, however, not improbable that we should here think rather of a *table altar*,[4] such as is actually found to Τύχη at Antioch.[5]

It is more difficult to decide what god or goddess is intended by *Měnî* (מְנִי), translated in the Revised Version *Destiny*.[6] The word would indeed be a natural translation of the Greek Μοῖρα;[7] but even assuming this to be correct, it yet remains doubtful whether *Měnî* denotes the same deity as *Gad* (according to the idiom known as complementary parallelism) or is distinct. In the earliest Greek literature Μοῖρα was regarded as single.[8] It is remarkable that Pindar (quoted by Pausanias, bk. viii, chap. xxvi. 3) regards Τύχη as one of the Μοῖραι. According to Pausanias (bk. i, chap. xix. 2) an inscription on the statue of Ἀφροδίτη ἐν Κήποις sets forth that Heavenly Aphrodite is the eldest of the Fates.

Similarly in chap. lxvi there are pretty clear indications that what is denounced is the heathenish worship of the days of Menelaus. The chapter consists of fragments composed at various times, but all within thirty years of the desecration of the Temple. Unfortunately the text of ver. 17 is somewhat mutilated, but there can be little doubt that the *gardens* are to be explained in the same manner as in

---

[1] Cf. Zech. ix. 5 ff.

[2] Baethgen, *Beiträge zur Semitischen Religionsgeschichte*, pp. 66, 76–80.

[3] Skinner, *Isaiah*, vol. ii, p. 215.

[4] See Reisch in Pauly-Wissowa, *Real-Encyclopädie*, vol. i, p. 1676.

[5] See British Museum Catalogue of Greek Coins, *Galatia, &c.*, plate xix. 9, xxii. 2.

[6] This sense is *implied*, though not *proved*, by the subsequent words ומנית אתכם לחרב. The verb in the latter clause certainly seems to be used according to the late, Aramaic, usage of מנה found in Jon. ii. 1, iv. 6–8; Job vii. 3; Dan. i. 5, 10, 11; 1 Chron. ix. 29; and perhaps Ps. lxi. 8.

The difficulty of determining the meaning of *Měnî* is increased by the fact that we have no evidence elsewhere of the existence of the word either as a proper name or as a common noun. This does not of course prove that such a noun did not exist. *Feminine* names from the same root are found both in Arabic and Aramaic, in the former as the name of a goddess, but this does not prove the existence of a *male* deity either among the Hebrews or Aramaeans.

[7] The ordinary text of the LXX renders גד (*Gad*) by δαιμόνιον and מני (*Měnî*) by Τύχῃ, but Field (*Hexapla*, p. 561) gives some evidence of the reverse order.

[8] See Roscher, *Lexikon der Griechischen und Römischen Mythologie*, art. Moira.

lxv. 3, and that the reference is to certain *mysteries* of which ceremonial purification was an important feature.¹ It would seem that these mysteries involved the eating of certain things which to a Jew were unclean; for the prophet continues, 'eating swine's flesh, and the abomination and the mouse.' It is not indeed actually stated that the unclean food is eaten in heathen *worship*, but the context seems to imply it. 'The dormouse (*Glis esculentus*), which the Talmud mentions under the name עכברא דברא (wild mouse) as a dainty bit with epicures, was fattened, as is well known, by the Romans in their glisaria.'² According to Maimonides the Harranians sacrificed field mice.³

If, however, the other references to heathenism are correctly explained of Greek customs, we must look for the eating of the mouse in the Greek area. Here we naturally think of *Apollo Smintheus*, who was worshipped at Alexandria Troas, and elsewhere. The present lecturer is again indebted to his friend Mr. A. B. Cook for calling his attention to a vase-painting,⁴ which represents a young man, kneeling apparently, on the δῖον κώδιον, the sacred fleece, stretching out his right hand towards a mouse or rat. Apparently it is a representation of some mystery.⁵ It is also noteworthy that in the collection of Imhoof-Blumer,⁶ there is a silver drachma of Alexander the Great, the reverse of which shows Zeus enthroned, with an eagle in his right hand, a sceptre in his left; the symbol in the field before him being a *mouse*. Silver staters of Nagidos struck about 374–333 B.C. have as obverse type Aphrodite enthroned, with a mouse as her attribute beneath her throne.⁷

The plight of the Ḥasîdîm seemed desperate. Unfortunately, of events, other than martyrdoms, at and immediately following the desecration of the Temple, we have no information. But three years later the writer of 1 Maccabees (iv. 38) describes the condition of the Temple as follows: 'And they saw the sanctuary laid desolate, and the altar profaned, and the gates burned up, and shrubs growing in

---

¹ Cf. Harrison, *Prolegomena to the Study of Greek Religion*, *passim*.
² Delitzsch on this passage.
³ Robertson Smith, *Religion of the Semites*, 2nd ed., p. 293.
⁴ See C. Lenormant et J. de Witte, *Élite des Monuments céramographiques*, vol. ii, p. 353, plate 104.
⁵ For the eating in mysteries of creatures otherwise sacred or taboo see Robertson Smith, *Religion of the Semites*, 2nd ed., p. 290 ff., and also Frazer, *Pausanias's Description of Greece*, vol. iii, p. 250.
⁶ See Imhoof-Blumer und Otto Keller, *Tier- und Pflanzenbilder auf Münzen und Gemmen*, p. 11, no. 6. plate 2. fig. 6.
⁷ See *British Museum Catalogue of Coins, Lycaonia, &c.*, p. 113 f., plate xx, 1 ff.

the court as in a forest, or as on one of the mountains, and the priests' chambers pulled down.' The description is remarkable, for, though the plundering of the Temple is recorded in 1 Macc. i. 21 ff., the previous account of Antiochus's doings at Jerusalem does not imply that either the Temple itself or the buildings in its precincts had been destroyed. Mr. E. R. Bevan comments on this description as follows : [1] 'Modern writers are apt to lose sight of something which the ancient Jewish writers did all they could to cover with oblivion—this Hellenizing Jewish community. It is one of the most interesting facts which Niese's *Kritik* has brought out, that in representing Jerusalem as desolate, and the Temple courts overgrown with wild shrubs in 165, the writer of 1 Maccabees is intentionally making a vacuum where really there was a Hellenistic population. The two accounts of what happened to the Temple, (1) that it was given over to heathen worship, (2) that it was forsaken, are in fact inconsistent.' Here, however, Mr. Bevan appears to have read into the description of the Temple more than the words necessarily imply.[2] Thus the statement that the sanctuary (ἁγίασμα) was desolate (ἠρημωμένον) need not be pressed to mean that the *main buildings* of the Temple were in actual ruins. Again, it is not said that *wild* shrubs were growing in the Temple courts. The most costly and beautiful trees or shrubs would be altogether anathema to those who held fast by the law of Deut. xvi. 21, and such people in describing a breach of this law would be likely to use somewhat exaggerated language. When an opponent of harvest-festival decorations complains nowadays that 'the church is turned into a greengrocer's shop', we do not take his words too literally. Inasmuch as the writer of 1 Maccabees distinctly states that only three years elapsed between the desecration of the Temple and its re-dedication, we can scarcely suppose that he intended people to believe that in so short a time *wild* shrubs sprang up in profusion on the top of a hill watered by so small a rainfall as Jerusalem possesses. There is no difficulty in supposing that trees had been planted by the Hellenizers and, possibly, that some of the very gardens which are denounced in Isa. lxv. 3 had been laid out in the Temple courts. In like manner we need not suppose that the priests' chambers had been left in ruins. They may have been pulled down to make room for something more beautiful; but to the Ḥasîdîm there was no beauty in anything heathenish. That the Temple did

---

[1] *House of Seleucus*, vol. ii, p. 298 f.

[2] Similarly in 1 Macc. iii. 45 the description of the desolation of Jerusalem, which is a *quotation* from the older scriptures, is not to be taken quite literally. The latter part of the verse indeed shows in what sense the first part must be understood.

suffer at this time seems clear from Ps. lxxiv. 4 ff.[1]; for though unfortunately the text of the Psalm is not very certain in places, ver. 7 makes it perfectly plain that some part of the sanctuary had been burnt. Perhaps in ver. 5 f. there is a reference to the stripping off of the Temple ornament mentioned in 1 Macc. i. 22. Now according to 2 Macc. i. 8 a gatehouse, apparently of the Temple, was burnt at the revolt of Jason (ἐνεπύρισαν τὸν πυλῶνα): and in 2 Macc. viii. 33 we read of 'those that had set the sacred gatehouses (τοὺς ἱεροὺς πυλῶνας) on fire'. It is unfortunately impossible from the uncertainty of the text in 2 Macc. viii. 33 to say when the burning of these gatehouses took place;[2] it may, however, be regarded as certain that more than one portion of the sacred enclosure had suffered from fire.

Here then we have a clue to the words which we now read in Isaiah lxiv. 10, 11: 'The holy cities are become a wilderness, Zion is become a wilderness, Jerusalem a desolation. Our holy and beautiful house,[3] where our fathers praised thee, is burned with fire.' The language of this passage is quite unsuitable to the time of Nebuchadnezzar; we can hardly suppose that any one in his days would have spoken of the cities of Judah as 'Jehovah's holy cities'. It is indeed conceivable that the Temple suffered in the attack upon Jerusalem implied in Neh. i. 3; but if so, Nehemiah's silence on the subject is inexplicable.[4]

When Antiochus Epiphanes set up in the Temple the image of Olympian Zeus, and placed on the great altar another altar on which swine were sacrificed, for the first time in a period of eight hundred years Jerusalem was left without a place of sacrifice to Jehovah. Even after Nebuchadnezzar had destroyed the Temple, people had continued to offer their sacrifices within the Temple area. But now there was no place in the whole world where they could worship

---

[1] For arguments for the Maccabæan date of this Psalm see Wellhausen's notes in the Polychrome Bible.

[2] If the damage had been done at the time of Jason's revolt one would have expected that it would have been repaired in Antiochus's reorganization of the Temple. It must, however, be remembered that Antiochus was occupied elsewhere, and that Menelaus was not the man to lay out his own wealth on the Temple. The damage *may* have been done wantonly by the agents of Antiochus as the opposition to the work which they were carrying out increased.

[3] The word 'house' does not necessarily denote the Temple proper. Thus in Jer. xli. 5, the Temple enclosure is called the house of the Lord, though the Temple itself was not standing.

[4] It is very questionable whether the very plain structure built by Zerubbabel (cf. Hag. ii. 3), as it was in the days of Nehemiah, could have been described as a 'beautiful house' (בֵּית תִּפְאֶרֶת). But in the days of Antiochus Epiphanes the Temple had been greatly restored by Simon the son of Oniah (Ecclus. l. 1 f.).

after the ancient manner the God of their fathers. It was small wonder if some people were perplexed as to what they ought to do. Probably there were some who argued that the Law merely affirmed the principle of a single sanctuary and laid down no injunction as to its situation. If during the forty years' wanderings the Lord's tabernacle had been pitched now in this place, now in that; if, before He made Jerusalem the place of His feet, He had made His name to dwell at Shiloh; would not the Jewish Church be justified, it might be argued, in building a Temple anywhere, provided that it built only *one* ? Was it not the divinely chosen priesthood, and the divinely appointed ritual that constituted the sanctuary rather than the locality ? Might not those who feared the Lord take refuge in Egypt or in some other place beyond the clutches of Antiochus ? Had not Isaiah himself declared that to Jehovah belonged the fullness of the whole earth ?

Of the intense yearning for sacrificial worship which was felt by those who were deprived of it, we have a beautiful illustration in Ps. lxiii : ' O God, thou art my God ; earnestly will I seek thee : my soul thirsteth for thee, my flesh longeth for thee, in a dry and weary land where no water is.'[1]

There is evidence that some at least of the Jews did argue in the way suggested above. For a younger Oniah (it cannot be determined whose son he was) fled to Egypt, and under the patronage of Ptolemy Philometor built a temple to Jehovah at Leontopolis in the nome of Heliopolis. Josephus, who relates the story in three places (*Wars of the Jews*, vii. 10 § 3; *Antiquities*, xii. 9 § 7, xiii. 3 § 1), places the flight of Oniah in the lifetime of Antiochus, but after the putting to death of Menelaus and the appointment of Alcimus ! Josephus is an untrustworthy guide in chronological matters, but it is probable that Oniah went to Egypt while the Temple at Jerusalem was still in the hands of the heathen. Josephus states (*Ant*. xiii. 3 § 3) that Oniah had a following among priests and Levites as well as among the laity.

But if there were some who thought that a temple might legitimately be built and sacrifices offered to Jehovah in the land of Egypt, there were others in Palestine who took a different view. To offer such worship as Oniah and his party contemplated was in their eyes to mistake the whole character of the religion of Israel, to lay stress on the outward and visible signs of Israel's sacraments rather than on the inward spiritual grace which in emergency could be independently received. It is probable that in Ps. l we have a protest against the project of building another temple which some of the perplexed

[1] Cf. also Ps. xlii, xliii.

Ḥasîdîm (note especially ver. 5) were inclined to favour. The psalmist declares that God's saints need not fear that He will refuse them on the score that they have ceased to sacrifice. What indeed is sacrifice, that God should require it? Will He eat the flesh of bulls, or drink the blood of goats? And similarly in Isa. lxvi. 1 ff., in words which set forth for all time an ideal of spiritual worship, the prophet ranges himself on the side of the psalmist: 'Thus saith the Lord, The heaven is my throne, and the earth is my footstool: what manner of house will ye build unto me? and what place shall be my rest? For all these things hath mine hand made, and so all these things came to be, saith the Lord: but to this man will I look, even to him that is poor and of a contrite spirit, and that trembleth at my word. He that killeth an ox is as he that slayeth a man; he that sacrificeth a lamb, as he that breaketh a dog's neck; he that offereth an oblation, as he that offereth swine's blood[1]; he that burneth frankincense, as he that blesseth an idol.'[2]

Perhaps it was the temptation to the Ḥasîdîm to look to Egypt at this time, either as a refuge or to furnish help against Antiochus, which caused the modification and re-editing of the old prophecies against Egypt contained in Isa. xxx, xxxi.

But if the faith of some failed, and they looked to Egypt for help, this was not the case with the Ḥasîdîm as a whole. The words which in Daniel iii. 17 are put into the mouth of Shadrach, Meshach, and Abednego accurately represent the temper of the Ḥasîdîm: 'If our God whom we serve be able to deliver us, from the burning fiery furnace and from thy hand, O king, He will deliver us. But if not, be it known unto thee, O king, that we will not serve thy gods, nor worship the golden image which thou hast set up.'

There is no power on earth that can compel a people with a faith such as this. Death and torture availed nothing to make the Ḥasîdîm eat of the King's meat or worship the image which he had set up. For God's sake they were killed all the day long, they were accounted as sheep for the slaughter. When they were attacked on the sabbath day, they perished unresistingly rather than profane the sabbath.[3] All their old ideas of retribution, of compensation to the righteous before death,[4] were shattered by the stern logic of events, and yet they were faithful. They were perplexed. They cried, as One still greater

---

[1] For swine's blood cf. Frazer, *Pausanias's Description of Greece*, vol. iii, pp. 277, 593.

[2] Therefore the people against whom the prophet's protest is directed are *not* idolaters, but Jews with a perverse idea of worship.

[3] 1 Macc. ii. 29 ff.   [4] Cf. e.g. Ecclus. xi. 25-28.

cried in His agony; 'My God, my God, why hast thou forsaken me?' They were mocked by their Hellenizing brethren, who hated them and cast them out for Jehovah's name's sake; who said 'Let the Lord be glorified, that we may see your joy' (Isaiah lxvi. 5). They were despised as fools, shunned as lepers; they were made the off-scouring of the world, a spectacle to angels and to men. But they knew that they were the true Israel, the Lord's chosen servant. The Lord God had revealed himself to them, and they were not rebellious, neither turned away backward. They gave their back to the smiters, and their cheeks to them that plucked off the hair: they hid not their face from shame and spitting. For they knew that the Lord Jehovah would help them: therefore they were not confounded: therefore they set their face like a flint, and knew that they would not be ashamed!¹

'And the Lord saw that there was no man, and wondered that there was none to interpose: therefore His own arm brought salvation unto Him; and His righteousness, it upheld Him.'²

It is impossible within the limits of these lectures to dwell on the events of the struggle.³ It must suffice to say that one family, the sons of Mattathias, whom we know as the Maccabees or the Hasmonaeans, from the name of their family, raised the standard of revolt, and exhorted the persecuted people to fight for their laws. It seemed a hopeless enterprise, but a war in the East demanded the attention of Antiochus, and he was unable to crush the rebellion. Within three years of the desecration of the Temple, Lysias, the general who had commanded the king's forces in Judaea, was compelled, probably owing to the death of Antiochus, to come to terms with the insurgents, by which they were allowed to take possession again of the Temple, and were granted religious freedom. But the Hasmonaeans, having once felt their power, were not disposed to be content with mere religious freedom. Moreover, it was impossible that the Ḥasîdîm should accept Menelaus, who still remained High Priest. Accordingly, the Hasmonaeans, who had set their heart on obtaining independence, continued the war. Whether they would have succeeded in their enterprise if the Syrian government had been united, is very doubtful; but during the long struggle which ensued there were generally rival claimants to the throne of Syria, and by throwing in their lot, now with one, now with another, the Hasmonaeans were able continually to obtain fresh concessions.

It is a remarkable testimony to the thoroughness of the work which

---

¹ See chap. l. 4 ff.   ² Chap. lix. 16.

³ The story is most admirably told in a popular form by Mr. E. R. Bevan in his book, *Jerusalem under the High Priests*.

had been done by Nehemiah in the fifth century B.C., that it was among the Jews alone of all the Palestinian nations that Hellenism met with any serious opposition. In the Maccabaean period the larger cities of Philistia, Edom, Moab, and 'Ammon appear to have possessed a very considerable Greek element side by side with the native population; and we may form some idea of the progress which Hellenism had made from the statement that towards the end of the second century the Edomites, who had originally been circumcised like the Jews, were compelled by John Hyrcanus to accept circumcision.[1] It is therefore not to be wondered at, if in the days of Antiochus Epiphanes, when the process of Hellenization was going on rapidly, the Jews dwelling in the non-Judaean cities of Palestine who refused to conform were exposed to more or less active persecution at the hands of their heathen neighbours.

As soon as the Hasmonaeans had got possession of the sanctuary of Mount Sion, they determined to rescue these Jews, and to take vengeance on the heathen for the sufferings which they had inflicted on them. Those who flattered themselves that Jehovah had been driven from His land were now to discover that He was in His holy Temple. There was 'a voice of tumult from the city, a voice from the Temple, a voice of the Lord that rendereth recompence to His enemies.'[2] In Galilee, Gilead, Ammon, Moab,[3] Edom, and Philistia the Maccabees took frightful vengeance on those who had oppressed the Jews in their midst. Campaigns against the Edomites are related in 1 Macc. v. 3, 65, and, although few details are given, we are able to form some idea of the horrors which were perpetrated from the account of what the Maccabees did in Gilead.[4]

In Isa. lxiii. 1-6 we have a song of triumph composed apparently

---

[1] See Josephus *Antiquities*, xiii. 9. § 1. We need not, of course, understand this statement to mean that circumcision had altogether died out in Edom, or that Hellenism had any strong hold on the Edomite peasantry; only that, whereas in the country districts of Judah Hellenism had encountered the most determined resistance, in Edom and the other neighbouring nations it was at all events tolerated. Where there was no opposition to the Hellenization that was being carried out in the cities, the agents of Antiochus would not be likely to investigate inquisitorially the religion of the country people.

[2] Isa. lxvi. 6.

[3] The details of the Moabite campaign are obscure, but Baean (1 Macc. v. 4 ff.; cf. 2 Macc. x. 18 ff.) is almost certainly in Moab, even if the probable identification of it with Baal-Meon is rejected. See *Encyclopaedia Biblica*, art. *Baal-Meon*.

[4] The statement of 1 Macc. v. 28 that at Bosora in Gilead Judas 'took the city, and slew all the males with the edge of the sword' bears a suspicious resemblance to the language of the Old Testament; but there is no reason to doubt that the slaughter was terrible.

at the time of one of these campaigns against Edom. The poet represents Jehovah as returning from Edom with garments dyed crimson in the blood of the Edomites.[1] It is to be noted that the punishment which the Edomites have suffered has been inflicted by the Jews alone. It is distinctly stated that none of the peoples had a hand in it.[2] We are therefore precluded from thinking of the Arab invasion of Edom in the fifth century B.C. Chap. xxxiv would seem to have been suggested by the same events.

To about the same period we should probably assign the short prophecy on Moab in xxv. 10 f. The author believes that when the hand of the Lord rests upon Zion, Moab will be trodden under the feet of the victorious Jews as straw is trodden under foot on the dung-heap, and will be incapable of rising.[3]

In 152 B.C., Jonathan, who had been allowed by King Demetrius to return to Jerusalem and to maintain a military force, was made High Priest by the rival king, Alexander Balas, who at the same time ennobled him; and two years later, after the defeat and death of Demetrius, he was appointed by Alexander governor of Judaea. Some two years later Demetrius II, the son of the former king of that name, appeared in Syria to claim his kingdom, and Jonathan on behalf of Alexander carried out a campaign against the Philistine cities which had espoused the cause of Demetrius. The triumph of the Jews was complete, and Jonathan was rewarded by having the city of Ekron assigned to him as a private possession.

It is probable that these campaigns, of which that against Philistia is almost certainly referred to in Zech. ix. 5-7, suggested the description of the expansion of the Jewish dominion which we find in Isa. xi, 14, composed, perhaps, some few years later: 'And they shall swoop down upon the flank of the Philistines on the west; together shall they spoil the children of the east: they will put forth their hand upon Edom and Moab; and the children of Ammon will obey them.'[4]

---

[1] The figure is suggested by the name *Bozrah,* which resembles the word for *vintage.*

[2] 'Of the peoples there was no man with me' (ver. 3).

[3] Moab is not thought of as swimming, but as lying on the ground in the attitude of a swimmer. A man who lies flat on his chest with arms and legs extended, with the foot of his enemy planted on his back, is in the most helpless position. The curious figure is, perhaps, derived ultimately from Mal. iv. 2, where the righteous are compared to fatted oxen (i.e. the most heavily treading animals in Jerusalem in Malachi's day) who tread heavily (*not* 'gambol') on the wicked as on ashes. The figure of stall-fed (i.e. fatted) oxen may have suggested the substitution of straw for ashes as well as the mention of the dung-heap; cf. Ps. lxxxiii 10.

[4] Cf. Ps. lxxxiii, lx. 8 (= cviii. 9).

LECTURE III

On the death of Alexander Balas in 145 B.C. Jonathan came to terms with Demetrius II, who, on consideration of the payment of 300 talents down, consented to make no further claim for tribute. In a few months, however, the infant son of Alexander Balas, known as Antiochus Dionysus, was proclaimed king by Tryphon, one of his father's generals; whereupon the Jews, deserting Demetrius, went over to his side. Tryphon confirmed to Jonathan the honours which had been conferred upon him by Alexander Balas, and at the same time appointed his brother Simon governor of the whole district 'from the Ladder of Tyre to the borders of Egypt'.[1] Shortly afterwards Jonathan, acting for Antiochus, carried out successful campaigns against the districts which remained loyal to Demetrius: we hear of operations in Philistia, beyond the Jordan as far as Damascus, and in Galilee. Suddenly, however, he was treacherously seized at Ptolemais by Tryphon, who thought that he was becoming too powerful (c. 143 B.C.). Simon, however, nothing daunted, strengthened the fortifications of Jerusalem; and seizing Joppa, which was already held by a Jewish garrison, he expelled the native population, and replaced it by Jews. It was an event which could not but stimulate the imagination of Jewish patriots. The possession of a harbour on the Mediterranean suggested the extension of Jewish influence to the west; the time was coming when the isles would wait for Jehovah, and the ships of Tarshish would bring back the dispersed of Israel laden with rich offerings to the sanctuary of the Lord.[2]

Tryphon attempted an invasion of Judaea, but found it impracticable. He, however, put Jonathan to death. Shortly afterwards Tryphon murdered the infant king, Antiochus Dionysus, whereupon Simon came to terms with Demetrius, who granted the Jews full exemption from all taxes or tribute to the Syrian government. 'The yoke of the heathen was taken away from Israel.'[3] In the following year (142-141) Gezer was taken by Simon, and made a Jewish stronghold; and finally, the Syrian garrison, which had hitherto held the citadel of Jerusalem, surrendered. On May 23, 141 B.C. Simon 'entered into it with praise and palm branches, and with harps, and with cymbals, and with viols, and with hymns, and with songs: because a great enemy was destroyed out of Israel'.[4]

It had been a long struggle, and yet from one point of view it might be described as very short. Almost at the beginning of the affliction it had been shown by whose means the deliverance should

---

[1] 1 Macc. xi. 59.　　[2] Cf. lx. 9, xlii. 4.
[3] 1 Macc. xiii. 41.　　[4] 1 Macc. xiii. 51.

come. Almost before Judaea had travailed she had brought forth; almost before her pain came, she had been delivered of a man child. The Jewish community, which had seemed in danger of utter extermination, had become a nation. An unheard-of thing had come to pass; a nation had been brought forth at once; 'for as soon as Zion travailed, she brought forth her children.' Jehovah had vindicated his righteousness: 'Shall I bring to the birth, and not cause to bring forth? saith the Lord: shall I that cause to bring forth shut the womb? saith thy God.'[1]

So marvellous were the successes which Simon and his brothers had gained, that, though Simon was not of the high-priestly family, 'the Jews and the priests were well pleased that Simon should be their leader and high priest *for ever*, until there should arise a faithful prophet.'[2]

No wonder that there was ecstatic joy in Jerusalem and Judaea as well as in other districts of Palestine where the Jews had been oppressed by the heathen. The old horror had passed away, and seemed like a hideous dream in the morning sunlight. In future men would 'muse on the terror' of the past, and would scarcely believe their eyes when they saw no more evidence of the presence of those who had exacted the tribute paid to the foreign oppressor.[3] Jehovah had, as it seemed, swallowed up for ever death from war and persecution, and He would wipe away tears from off all faces, and the rebuke of His people He would take away from off all the land.[4]

It is, in all probability, to this period that we must assign the magnificent outburst of triumph in chap. ix. The land that was sore afflicted had seen a great light: the Way of the Sea (i.e. the Philistine plain, the plain of Sharon, and the coast to the north), the district beyond Jordan, Galilee of the nations, had been brought to honour in that they were now to some extent occupied by Jews who were free to worship God according to the law of Israel. It seemed an earnest of a more complete restoration of the land of Israel. The Lord had multiplied the exultation; He had increased the joy: for the yoke of the heathen was broken. Israel had travailed and had brought forth a man child. The government had come upon his back: he had proved himself a 'marvellous designer' (פֶּלֶא יוֹעֵץ), a 'mighty warrior' (אֵל גִּבּוֹר); his dynasty would be a permanent one, a 'father in perpetuity' (אֲבִי עַד) to Israel; and to crown the other blessings, war would give way to peace: the ruler of the future would be a 'prince of peace' (שַׂר שָׁלוֹם).

[1] Isa. lxvi. 7 ff.; cf. lx. 22.   [2] 1 Macc. xiv. 41.
[3] Cf. Isa. xxxiii. 18.   [4] Cf. xxv. 7.

This view of the date of Isa. ix. 1–7 is made probable not only by the fact that no other period is known to us to which every clause of the prophecy is applicable, but also by an archaeological detail. In describing the abolition of war and all associated with it the prophet writes, according to the literal meaning of the Hebrew, 'For every boot of noisily booted one, and garment rolled (? read 'stained' i. e. מְגֹאָלָה for מְגוֹלָלָה) in blood shall be made into a bonfire, into fuel of fire.' The boots here contemplated are evidently those which make a noise as the wearer walks, i. e. heavy nailed boots as distinct from the light shoes worn by orientals. Now high nailed boots were a characteristic of the Macedonian soldiery, and were still worn by the Syrian soldiers in the second century B. C.[1] In Theocritus, *Id.* xv. 6. Gorgo the Syracusan is represented as exclaiming on the occasion of a military procession in Alexandria, 'Everywhere military boots!' (κρηπῖδες). Isaiah in speaking (v. 27) of the equipment of the Assyrians uses the ordinary Hebrew word for *shoe* (נַעַל).[2]

The rule of Simon as a virtually independent prince raised the hope of a complete restoration of the Kingdom. Already, probably at the time of Jonathan's successes in Philistia, a Hebrew prophet had predicted that the Jews would have a king of their own: 'Rejoice greatly, O daughter of Zion; shout, O daughter of Jerusalem: behold, thy king will come unto thee: one just and victorious; and (withal) poor and riding upon an ass, yea on a choice he-ass the foal of an ass.'[3] This prediction now seemed likely to be fulfilled. Those who had agonized under a foreign tyrant might now hope to see 'a king in his beauty', and to 'behold a far stretching land'.[4] Now they might hope for a settled government founded in righteousness which would be a protection to the poor and helpless: 'Behold, a king will reign in righteousness, and princes will rule in justice. And one will be as a hiding place from the wind, and as a covert from the tempest; as rivers of water in a dry place, as the shadow of a great rock in a weary land.'[5]

We know that it is the will of our Heavenly Father to make perfect through suffering. In the Jewish Church at the close of the Mac-

---

[1] See Darenberg and Saglio: *Crepida, Crepidula*, Κρηπίς.

[2] For a fuller discussion of the whole passage see the present lecturer's article in the *Journal of Theological Studies*, vol. vii, p. 321 ff.

[3] Zech. ix. 9. Note the future 'WILL come' (not 'cometh'). The looked-for king is to be *poor*, i.e. poor in an official sense, he will belong to the Ḥasidim. He is represented as riding not on a horse, the symbol of war, but as the Judges of Israel rode in the days of old on the ass, the ordinary riding animal of the country.

[4] Isa. xxxiii. 17.   [5] Isa. xxxii. 1 f.; cf. also xi. 1 ff.

cabaean struggle we see one fruit of its long discipline.[1] It has at length learnt the meaning of martyrdom. Those who had once set the Ḥasîdîm at nought now recognized their true greatness, and perceived that they, and they alone, could rightly claim to be the true Israel. It was not their own apostasy but that of their brethren which had brought their sufferings upon them; yet their brethren who had opposed them, or had, at best, been passive spectators of their sufferings, had been partakers in the benefits which by their constancy they had won. In Isaiah lii. 13 – liii we have, in all probability, the meditation of Israel as a whole upon the sufferings of the Ḥasîdîm, the true Church of Israel, Jehovah's true servant. The passage has, indeed, been frequently understood to be an *ideal* description of the means by which a coming deliverer will achieve the salvation of his people; but such an interpretation does violence to Hebrew grammar. A careful study of the tenses of the verbs here used *shows with absolute certainty that the suffering of the Lord's servant is an accomplished fact*, and that this suffering has already issued in the deliverance of the nation, from which still further blessings are looked for in the future.

By their steadfastness in a time of apostasy the Ḥasîdîm had proved themselves to be the true Israel; but further, it was owing to them that the national existence of Israel was preserved, so that it could be said of them in the days of Simon that they had been chosen as Jehovah's servant 'to raise up the tribes of Jacob, and to restore the preserved of Israel'.[2] But this was not all; when the yoke of the heathen was taken away from Israel, there was opened up a prospect of a wider Judaism, the influence of which would be seen throughout the world. Hitherto it had been impossible for the Jews of the Dispersion, whether in Egypt or in Assyria, i. e. the Seleucid empire,[3] to come up to Jerusalem to keep the feasts. But now all such difficulties would be a thing of the past. Jehovah, of whom it had been said long before that He would have a highway through the desert

---

[1] This is true of the Church as a whole, but we must not, of course, imagine that all the Jews were equally purified in the furnace of affliction. The utterances of this period are not all equally in harmony with the spiritual teaching of the book of Jonah. The voice which speaks, for example, in Isa. lxiii. 1 ff., and which so often finds expression in the books of Maccabees, is not the same as that which speaks in Isa. liii, which represents more truly the faith of those whose martyrdom is escribed in 1 Macc. ii. 29 ff. It is doubtful whether for the Maccabaean leaders themselves any virtue can be claimed except personal courage and a certain amount of patriotism, largely mingled, however, if not swallowed up, with personal ambition.

[2] Isa. xlix. 6.

[3] For this use of Assyria (אַשּׁוּר), cf. Ezra vi. 22, Isa. xi. 16, xix. 23 ff.

(xl. 3 ff), would dry up the tongue of the Egyptian Sea, and divide the Euphrates into seven streams, so that men should go over dryshod.[1] By the removal of physical obstacles we are, of course, to understand the removal of political obstacles. It was felt that when there was no longer any hindrance to worshipping the Lord in His Temple, the teaching committed to Israel would have its perfect work: 'out of Zion would go forth the law, and the word of the Lord from Jerusalem.'[2] Then Jehovah's servant Israel, having raised up the tribes of Jacob, would be a light to the Gentiles, and would bring Jehovah's salvation to the end of the earth.[3]

In Zechariah xiv, a passage which was probably composed about the time of Simon's High-priesthood, the stream of living water which Ezekiel (xlvii) had described as flowing eastward from the Temple to the healing of the district east of it, is duplicated (ver. 8), so that it flows not only eastward to the regeneration of the heathen world of Asia, but also westward to the regeneration of the heathen world which lay round the Mediterranean. The stream of living water is the revelation committed to Israel. Perhaps, however, there were some who contemplated the future missionary work of Israel with serious misgivings, and thought that contact with heathenism involved danger to Israel itself. It may be that they argued that if a river issued from Jerusalem ships of heathenism might, so to speak, sail up to its source. But the prophet to whom we owe the exquisite passage Isaiah xxxiii. 13-24 had no such fears. He declared that on the broad rivers and streams of living water which would issue from Zion there would go no galley with oars, neither would any warship sail thereby.[4] It was felt that the peace of Jerusalem would be unbroken, for all nations would recognize its pre-eminence. They would beat their swords into plowshares, and their spears into pruninghooks: nation would not lift up sword against nation, neither would they learn war any more.[5]

At the outset of the Maccabaean struggle, when the Jews were opposed by the great empire of Antiochus, composed as it was of 'all peoples, nations, and languages', it had seemed as though all the nations of the world were gathered together to fight against Jerusalem. This is the picture which is represented to us in Zech. xiv. 2.[6] But in the High-priesthood of Simon the victory which the Lord had gained was believed to be final. Those who had fought against Him

---

[1] Isa. xi. 15.   [2] Isa. ii. 3.   [3] Isa. xlix. 6.
[4] This must not be understood to mean that there is here any direct reference to Zech. xiv. The thought of this stream of water was probably common at this period; cf. Ps. xlvi. 4, Joel iii. 18.
[5] Cf. ii. 2 ff.   [6] Cf. Joel iii. 11 ff.

and whose dead bodies lay unburied outside Jerusalem, slowly vanishing as worms and bonfires did their work, would never again, like the bones in Ezekiel's vision, 'arise and stand upon their feet an exceeding great army', to imperil the name and the seed of Israel. 'Their worm would not die, neither would their fire be quenched,' and those who assembled to worship in Jerusalem [1] would recognize in their destruction the final triumph of the Lord.[2]

We have seen that during the time that Palestine was subject to Ptolemaic rule, when the Jewish colonies in Egypt were increased by fresh migrations from Judaea, the Jews of Egypt were brought into closer relations with their Palestinian brethren. These relations were doubtless interrupted when the Seleucid kings of Syria gained possession of Palestine. But when Judaea had become virtually independent, it was hoped not only that the Jews of Egypt would be able without let or hindrance to keep the feasts at Jerusalem, but also that the Egyptians themselves would be converted, and would accompany them;[3] and that Egyptian opposition to Jehovah's people would so entirely disappear, that Egypt would become to some extent a Jewish colony speaking the Hebrew language.[4] There seemed reason to hope indeed that Egypt would, so to speak, have its Jerusalem, and that, as the worship of the Temple had been brought into thorough harmony with the Law, so Leontopolis, the place where Oniah had established a schismatical Jewish worship, would in like manner be made to conform with the Law of the One Sanctuary.[5] The altar built by Oniah need not be destroyed, but might be left— like the altar built by the Reubenites, Gadites, and half the tribe of Manasseh—as a witness in Egypt to the fact that Jehovah alone is God.[6] Egypt indeed should be recognized as Jehovah's land, and a pillar on the frontier should witness to the fact, as the pillars which had once been set up on Mt. Ebal [7] witnessed to His being the God

---

[1] Cf. xxv. 6.   [2] Cf. lxvi. 22-24.
[3] Cf. Zech. xiv. 16-19.   [4] Isa. xix. 18.

[5] The statement that 'one city shall be called the city of Piety' (reading with Prof. F. C. Burkitt, *Journal of Theological Studies*, vol. i. p. 568 f., חסד piety for הרם destruction) can only mean that one city in Egypt will conform to the ideal of the Ḥasidim. This probably means that, as the Ḥasidim of Judaea had reformed the worship of the Temple, so the Ḥasidim of Egypt would reform the worship of Leontopolis.

[6] Cf. Joshua xxii.

[7] Cf. Deut. xxvii. It is probable that the prophet has in view the narratives of Joshua xxii and Deut. xxvii. It is difficult to suppose that any section of the Church at Jerusalem was prepared to tolerate sacrificial worship at Leontopolis. Certainly all other passages insist in the strongest terms on the unique character of Jerusalem.

of Samaria. Finally Egypt and Assyria (i.e. the Seleucid empire), being converted to the Lord by the Jews dwelling in their midst, would be as blessed as Israel itself, 'for that the Lord of hosts had blessed them, saying, Blessed be Egypt my people, and Assyria the work of my hands, and Israel mine inheritance.'

In the calm which for a while succeeded the storm, it seemed as if the reign of war had come to an end, and the reign of peace had begun. No longer would Jew oppress his brother Jew: Hellenizers and Ḥasîdîm would live in peace together. 'The wolf and the lamb would feed together, and the lion would eat straw like the ox.'[1] No longer would men live in constant fear of danger and oppression, of which darkness is the natural symbol:[2] 'Thy sun shall no more go down, neither shall thy moon withdraw itself: for the Lord shall be thine everlasting light, and the days of thy mourning shall be ended.'[3] Old things appeared to have passed away : all things had become new. The Lord was creating, as it were, a new heaven and a new earth, an earth which should be full of the knowledge of the Lord, as the waters cover the sea.

We have seen that the opposition to Hellenism came from the country districts of Judah rather than from Jerusalem, and that the leader of apostasy was the High Priest. Of the part taken by the inferior clergy who ministered in the Temple at the time of its desecration we have no information. No priests are mentioned among those who suffered for their adherence to the Law,[4] and there is no indication that either Jason, Menelaus or Alcimus encountered any opposition from the clergy of the Temple. We are told, indeed, that for the purification of the Temple, Judas chose 'blameless priests such as had pleasure in the law ;'[5] but these, like the family of Mattathias, may well have had their homes outside Jerusalem. In any case Menelaus and Alcimus, though they might find it expedient to conform to the main essentials of the ritual law, were not the men to feel any great enthusiasm for the Scriptures which the Ḥasîdîm so dearly prized.

At the outset of the struggle an attempt had been made to destroy all copies of the Law ;[6] and, since we cannot suppose that the king's officers would be likely to discriminate between the Law proper and other sacred books, it is evident that there must have been a wholesale destruction of all Scriptures and writings associated with them.

---

[1] Chap. lxv. 25 ; cf. xi. 6.   [2] Cf. Zech. xiv. 6, 7.   [3] Chap. lx. 20.
[4] Unless it be in 1 Macc. iii. 51. But the writer here is so obviously trying to write in a scriptural strain, that his words are not very convincing.
[5] 1 Macc. iv. 42.   [6] 1 Macc. i. 56 f.

It is probable that when the Temple was given up to the Maccabees there were no whole copies of the Scriptures remaining in Jerusalem. We read[1] indeed of the opening of the book of the Law, but this is at Mizpah, not Jerusalem.

Further it must be remembered that, although, in all probability, the Temple had originally possessed copies of the Scriptures, it is extremely unlikely that it had ever been a place for the study of the Scriptures. It existed for sacrificial and ritual worship, not for instruction. It was in the synagogues, and probably the synagogues of the country towns and districts, that the scribes' influence was paramount. It is therefore likely that the first efforts to replace the Scriptures which had been so ruthlessly destroyed would be made, not by the priests of Jerusalem, but by the scribes of the synagogues, more especially the country synagogues.

But it is unlikely that even after the re-dedication of the Temple the influence of the scribes was much felt at Jerusalem, at all events for a considerable time. Neither Menelaus, who remained High Priest, nor his successor Alcimus, was likely to further any attempt to restore a very un-Hellenic Bible, and even the ' blameless priests ' chosen by Judas may have cared more for orthodox ritual than for the more spiritual aspect of religion. There is no probability that the scribes would have been able to influence Jerusalem before the High-priesthood of Jonathan, and it is doubtful whether, at any rate at first, Jonathan's appointment was acceptable to the Ḥasîdîm. Those who had been willing to accept Alcimus on the ground that he was a priest of the seed of Aaron[2] may have looked askance at one who, though of priestly family, had no claim to the High-priesthood, and was regarded as a soldier rather than as a priest. At all events, we hear of no popular confirmation of Jonathan's High-priesthood as in the case of Simon.[3]

But by the time of Simon's succession to the High-priesthood the feelings of the majority of the Jewish nation had undergone a change. Much which at the outset would have been opposed both by the Ḥasîdîm and by the Hellenists seemed to have found justification in the course of events. If the Ḥasîdîm did not find in Simon all that they could have desired, they could not shut their eyes to the fact that he and his brothers had won for them freedom to worship God, and that his rule promised greater advantages to the nation than it had enjoyed since the days of the kings. And in like manner, when the nationalist movement among the Jews had been so successful that Greek kings had been glad to come to terms with the Jewish leaders,

[1] 1 Macc. iii. 48. [2] 1 Macc. vii. 13, 14. [3] 1 Macc. xiv. 41, 46.

those who had once sought to escape from a social stigma by the adoption of Hellenism no longer had cause to be ashamed of their nationality. Moreover, inasmuch as the national existence of the Jews had been saved rather by the struggles of the inhabitants of the country districts of Judah than by the action of the citizens of Jerusalem, the former, who had once been despised as provincials, now felt that they were on an equality with the latter. The Lord had saved the homes of Judah first, that the glory of the house of David and the glory of the inhabitants of Jerusalem might not be magnified above Judah.[1]

And with the change in the position of the Ḥasîdîm there had come a change in their attitude towards those who had opposed them. If in the bitterness of the conflict they had prayed that the Hellenists might be blotted out of the book of the living, and not be written with the righteous,[2] now they felt that repentance would atone for all that was past: 'Let the wicked forsake his way, and the unrighteous man his thoughts: and let him return unto the Lord, and he will have mercy upon him; and to our God, for he will abundantly pardon.'[3]

It is therefore not unreasonable to suppose that in the High-priesthood of Simon the scribes possessed a far greater influence than for many years previously; and that Jerusalem having turned 'to the law and to the testimony', there was a demand in the Holy City for copies of the Scriptures. It is certainly probable that, if such a demand existed at this time, it could not be supplied from Jerusalem. Those who had in view the redaction of an authoritative edition of the Scriptures would be compelled to seek among the country synagogues such manuscripts as had escaped the fury of the persecutors. There would probably be few, if any, *whole* copies of the Scriptures which Ben Sira had known; but together with the torn and mutilated rolls which the synagogues had saved from the general destruction there would doubtless be fragments of more recent date, psalms and hymns and spiritual songs, utterances of despair or songs of victory, in which the struggling people had poured out their souls to God. We cannot tell from how wide an area manuscripts were gathered up;[4] it may be that Galilee as well as Judaea contributed its writings.

---

[1] Zech. xii. 7.   [2] Ps. lxix. 28.   [3] Isa. lv. 7.

[4] Some evidence of a composition, or at all events an editing, at a distance from Jerusalem may be found in the statement of Zech. xiv. 4, that the Mount of Olives is 'before Jerusalem on the east'. Even if this be a gloss, which is by no means certain, it is a gloss which no inhabitant of Jerusalem would be likely to add.

In Ben Sira's great list of famous men of Israel it is said of Isaiah[1] that 'he saw by an excellent spirit what should come to pass at the last; and he comforted them that mourned in Sion.' If, then, Isaiah was honoured as the prophet of consolation, and as one who had received special knowledge of 'what should come to pass at the last', it is little wonder that the scribes added to the collection of prophecies which already bore Isaiah's name others which seemed to be a worthy expression of his spirit. The Canon of the Prophets had already been decided so far as the names and number of the prophetical books were concerned, but not as to the contents of the books. As it had been possible in the age following Nehemiah's reforms to add to the words of Isaiah of Jerusalem the utterances of a Babylonian Jewish prophet, so it was possible now to add to this great book of consolation the utterances of some of those who were entitled to be reckoned among Israel's greatest prophets, although they did not claim any such title. It is, no doubt, impossible to determine precisely what principles of arrangement guided the latest redactors, though here and there we can, perhaps, discover their reasons for placing a late passage with earlier compositions. Thus, for example, ix. 1–7 was probably placed in its present context because it seemed a fitting sequel to the Immanuel prophecy. It is possible that the various compositions in the section xxiv–xxvii had been collected into one roll in a synagogue before they became the property of the Church generally. How long the process of redaction lasted we cannot say, but there is certainly no great difficulty in supposing that it may have been finished in, or shortly after, the year 140 B.C.[2]

We have seen that, so far as we are able to form any opinion from the scanty evidence available, the Jewish community in Egypt did not in all probability possess the Law till the third century B.C., when it was translated into Greek. It is certainly unlikely that the prophetical books were known in Egypt at an earlier date than the Law; for the formation of the *nucleus* of the second portion of the Hebrew Canon is probably to be regarded as the outcome of

---

[1] Ecclus. xlviii. 22 ff.

[2] It may perhaps be felt by some that the arguments adduced to support so late a date for the book of Isaiah would have equal force in bringing down its composition to a still later period. Thus it might be urged that John Hyrcanus treated the Edomites more severely than Judas. But the inference which is naturally drawn from the language of such passages as lxiii. 4 f. is that the persecution of the Jews by the Edomites has continued *unchecked* until Jehovah's great act of vengeance which the prophet here describes; and this inference, though it is in accordance with the time of Judas, does not suit the time of John Hyrcanus.

LECTURE III 79

the work which the school of Ezra had accomplished in combining the law of the Church of Palestine with that of the Jewish community in Babylonia. Even if Jewish immigrants had taken with them to Egypt copies of the earlier prophetical Scriptures, these must have been in Hebrew, of which most Jews in Egypt seem to have had little or no knowledge. Now inasmuch as in the days of Ben Sira there appear to have been fifteen prophetical books (exclusive of those which in the Jewish Canon are regarded as the Earlier Prophets) it is, perhaps, not impossible that a translation of some of these books may have been made at the same time as the translation of the Law. But though we cannot say that such a translation was not made, there is no evidence that it was. In the first place there can be no question that in the third century B.C. the Law had the pre-eminence among the Scriptures in the Church of Palestine; and in order to carry out so great a reform as the imposition of the Law on the Jewish community in Egypt, the reformers would probably at first content themselves with insisting only upon what they considered to be essential. It is moreover evident from a study of the style of the Septuagint translation that the version was not all completed at one time.[1] Further, the position of the book of Daniel in the Greek Bible is in itself a weighty argument against the supposition that the Egyptian Jews received the Prophets with the Pentateuch. For if the Jewish community in Egypt had already possessed the Canon of the Prophets for a considerable length of time when the book of Daniel was translated into Greek, it is extremely improbable that this book, which the Palestinian Church placed on a lower level of canonicity, would have been admitted into its present place. The evidence, so far as it goes, points to the conclusion that the Jewish Church in Egypt received the Scriptures, other than the Pentateuch, piece-meal; in much the same way as a modern Church planted in a heathen country receives the Scriptures in instalments, as the missionaries are able to translate them. Finally, the existence in the Greek Canon of books which the Palestinian Church did not accept as canonical leads us to the same conclusion. If, for example, Ben Sira's book was translated into Greek about the time that Greek versions of the canonical Scriptures were being made, we can understand its reception into the Canon in Egypt.

We have seen that the book of Isaiah contains passages which may have been composed as late as about 141 B.C., and therefore, if this view be correct, the Greek version of the book cannot have been made

[1] See Ryle, *Canon of the Old Testament*, p. 90.

before this date. We have now to inquire what is the latest date to which it can be assigned. It is evident from the Prologue to the book of Ecclesiasticus that the translator believed his grandfather Jesus to have been acquainted with 'the Law and the Prophets and the other books of the Fathers'; which is a clear indication that he himself was acquainted with a threefold division of the Canon, though it does not prove, at all events in the case of the last division, that the Canon was finally closed. We cannot, however, argue that the author of the Prologue to Ecclesiasticus found the Law and the Prophets and the other books mentioned by him all already translated into Greek when he arrived in Egypt; but only that translations of them had been completed before his own version of his grandfather's book was ready, which, it is implied, was some time, perhaps a very considerable time, after his arrival in 132 B.C.

There is therefore no reason for assuming that the translation of the book of Isaiah into Greek was begun in Egypt before, at the earliest, 132 B.C., and this would give ample time for the final redaction of the Hebrew book. It is, however, possible, as Mr. Hart has suggested,[1] that συγχρονίσας means 'I stayed in Egypt so long as king Euergetes reigned'; which, if Euergetes be Euergetes II, brings us down to the year 117 B.C.

Mr. Hart, indeed, endeavours to identify Euergetes with Euergetes I, understanding by 'the thirty-eighth year' the thirty-eighth year of the preceding king, Ptolemy Philadelphus, who died before its completion; but his chief argument for this somewhat difficult interpretation of the date is not altogether convincing. He maintains that 'unless the unanimous testimony of all known historians be set aside as proceeding from a conspiracy of malicious liars, the conclusion, that any sane Jew came to Egypt in this reign and was able to remain there until he had rendered some Jewish book or books into Greek is incredible'.[2]

But, as a matter of fact, those who are commonly reputed sane, both Jews and Gentiles, do not infrequently settle in places which appear to offer little attraction and much danger. If Ptolemy Euergetes II persecuted many Alexandrian Jews who had favoured his brother's cause, we are not compelled to believe that all Jews as such were in danger even in Alexandria. There is no evidence that there was at this time a general persecution of the Jews in Egypt: certainly all the Jews were not turned out of Egypt, for the Temple at Leontopolis continued down to the time of Josephus.[3] Mr. Hart indeed says, 'It is

---

[1] Hart, *Ecclesiasticus in Greek*, p. 259.   [2] Ibid., p. 254.
[3] See Josephus, *Wars of the Jews*, book vii, chap. x. 2, 3.

possible of course—all things are possible—that in some secluded corner of Egypt the work of the translators of the Scripture went forward aided by such recruits from Palestine, in spite, let us say, of Ptolemy Philopator and now of Ptolemy Physcon'; [1] but he adds, 'But our writer speaks of publishing the book, and this involves a publicity which would have been disastrous.'

Yet books both Jewish and Christian have been published in times of persecution, sometimes, indeed, because of the persecution. Certainly if in the reign of Euergetes II the Jews were persecuted *as Jews*, those who knew the inspiring influence of the Hebrew Prophets and Psalmists would have the strongest inducement to encourage their oppressed brethren in Egypt by bringing to them also a knowledge of the teaching which had enabled the Palestinian Jews to triumph over their heathen persecutors.

In the absence of any conclusive evidence for the early date commonly postulated for the Septuagint translation of the Prophets and Hagiographa, and in view of the fact that from the known circumstances of the period beginning about 176 B.C. and ending in the High-priesthood of Simon it is possible to find a satisfactory explanation of every translatable clause, not of one passage of Scripture only, but of many, which cannot be satisfactorily explained from the known circumstances of any other period, it is surely not unreasonable to assert that a Maccabaean date is proved for these passages in so far as proof in a matter of this sort is at all possible.

And finally, a protest must be made against the all-too-common assumption that those who assign any portion of the Old Testament to so late a date are to be regarded as 'wild' or 'sceptical'. If there is any scepticism involved in the critical study of Holy Scripture, it is shared by all who deviate, be it ever so little, from the traditional view. If, for example, the assignment of portions of the book of Isaiah to the close of the Persian period (i.e. some four centuries later than the time of Isaiah the son of Amoz) be compatible with faith—and who in these days will dare to assert that it is not?—why should it be supposed that the assignment of these portions to the Maccabaean period is the outcome of scepticism? The history of the change in religious thought during the past generation should surely be a lesson to us not to set up in our hearts an idol of orthodoxy, albeit critical orthodoxy, but to follow the example of the Jews of Beroea,[2] and to search the Scriptures to see what they really teach. Inasmuch as things which thirty years ago were not so much as

---

[1] Op. cit. p. 257. [2] Acts xvii. 11.

whispered in the ears of the most promising students of Theology in the English Universities, at all events at Cambridge, are now proclaimed on the very housetops, and are set forth in books intended for school use, it is surely not over bold to maintain that there may still be many questions connected with the Old Testament on which the last word has not yet been spoken. In any case, with honest, patient, and reverent study there will come a fuller revelation of Him who spake by the Prophets; for 'the grass withereth, the flower fadeth; but the word of our God shall stand for ever'.

CLASSIFICATION

OF THE SECTIONS OF THE BOOK OF ISAIAH

THE following list is an attempt to classify roughly for the convenience of readers the various sections of the book of Isaiah according to the periods to which *in their present form* they appear most naturally to belong. Thus sections which, though they may be composed of genuine Isaianic phrases, are more suitable as they stand to the period of the Maccabees than to that of Isaiah will be found classified with the compositions of the second century B.C. It is not impossible, indeed, that comparatively early prophecies of considerable extent may have been modified at various dates to meet the exigencies of later times; and in cases of this sort the assignment of such passages in their present form to a late date must not be understood as a denial of the possibility of an early origin. The book of Daniel, in which Nebuchadnezzar and his successors are represented in the *rôle* which in the time of the author of the book was filled by Antiochus Epiphanes, shows how natural it was to a Judæan prophet— for we need not grudge the name of prophet to the author of the book of Daniel—to modify denunciations of Babylon to suit the circumstances of his own age. Indeed, at a much later date we find a similar method of treating existing Scriptures. Thus the Targum Yerushalmi gives the following rendering of Numbers xxiv. 19: 'And he will destroy and bring to an end the remnant that is left of Constantinople the guilty city.' Nor is there any difficulty in imagining the combination of passages of entirely different *provenance*. Students of the Synoptic Gospels, at all events, will admit that early Jewish editors dealt with their documents in the freest manner possible. In the book of Isaiah, as it has come down to us, and, indeed, in other books also, we have to a great extent what we are accustomed to in Handel's Oratorio *The Messiah*, in which Isaiah xl. 11 is immediately followed by S. Matthew xi. 28; the two passages being so welded together by the melody, that the description of the ideal Shepherd at once suggests the invitation, 'Come unto Him.' We must never lose sight of the fact that the compilers of the books of the Prophets were actuated not by any archæological interest in the sayings of the holy men of old, but by a desire to provide spiritual edification for their own time.

This consideration will serve also as a warning against imagining that those passages which manifestly refer to the time of Isaiah must have come down to us in all respects unchanged.

PASSAGES WHICH MAY BE ASSIGNED TO ISAIAH THE SON OF AMOZ.[1]

i. 2–23.	ix. 8–21.
ii. 6–21.	x. 1–19, 28–32.
iii.	xiv. 28–32.
iv. 1.	xvii. 1–3.
v.	xx.
vi.	xxii.[2]
vii.	xxviii.[3]
viii. 1–18.	xxxi.

PASSAGES WHICH MAY BE ASSIGNED TO THE TIME OF CYRUS.

xiii.	xliv. 9–20, 24–28.
xiv. 1–27.	xlv. 1–13.
xxi.[4]	xlvi.
xl.	xlvii.
xli. 1–7, 21–29.	xlviii. 12–15, 20, 21.
xliii.[5]	

PASSAGES WHICH MAY BE ASSIGNED TO THE PERIOD BETWEEN NEBUCHADNEZZAR AND ALEXANDER THE GREAT, BUT WHICH CANNOT BE DATED PRECISELY.

xv.	xxxvii.
xvi. 1–12.	xxxviii.[7]
xxxvi.	xxxix.

A PASSAGE WHICH MAY BE ASSIGNED TO THE TIME OF ALEXANDER THE GREAT (332 B.C.).

xxiii. 1–14.

---

[1] N.B. No attempt is made in this list to analyse sections which, though probably Isaianic, are not homogeneous, nor to arrange the sections in exact chronological order. The division of the chapters is that of the *English* Bible.

[2] In the main. But in the earlier part of the chapter the text is too corrupt to speak with certainty, and in verses 20–5 we have additions to the original prophecy, which were perhaps made successively somewhat later.

[3] Verses 23–9 probably belong to a later age, viz. the period of the development of the Wisdom literature, i.e. the third or second century B.C.

[4] With the doubtful exception of verses 13–17.

[5] In the main; but with considerable later modifications.

[6] In the main.

[7] The psalm (verses 9–20) is an insertion from another source, and may be considerably later.

THE BOOK OF ISAIAH

PASSAGES WHICH MAY BE ASSIGNED TO THE SECOND CENTURY B.C.

i. 24–31.	xli. 8–20.
ii. 1–5, 22.[1]	xlii.
iv. 2–6.	xliv. 1–8, 21–23.
viii. 19–22.[2]	xlv. 14–25.
ix. 1–7.	xlviii. 1–11, 16–19, 22.
x. 20–27, 33, 34.	xlix.
xi.	l.
xii.	li.
xvi. 13, 14.	lii.
xvii. 4–14.	liii.
xviii.[3]	liv.
xix.	lv.
xxiii. 15–18.	lvi.
xxiv.	lvii.[4]
xxv.	lviii.
xxvi.	lix.
xxvii.	lx.
xxix.	lxi.
xxx.	lxii.
xxxii.	lxiii.
xxxiii.	lxiv.
xxxiv.	lxv.
xxxv.	lxvi.

[1] But possibly this verse is still later.
[2] Probably.
[3] Obscure from corruption of the text. Possibly based on a genuine Isianic prophecy.
[4] Except verse 5.

GENERAL INDEX

'*n*' refers to the notes at the bottom of the pages.

Agade, 32.
Ahaz rebuked by Isaiah, 12.
— summoned to Damascus, 16.
— name incorrectly read for that of King of Assyria, 18 *n*.
— reign of, 20, 21.
Alcimus, 64, 75, 76.
Alexander Balas, rival of King Demetrius, 68.
— — death of, 69.
Alexander the Great, 35 *n*.
— conquers Asia Minor, Phoenicia, and Palestine, 36 f.
— effect of his coming on Jerusalem, 38 f.
— policy of, 49.
— completes Heroum, 58.
Alexandria proclaims Ptolemy Euergetes king, 52.
— besieged by Antiochus Epiphanes, 53, 54.
— Jewish inhabitants of, 80.
Amaziah, 10.
Amel Marduk, accession of, 29.
Ammon submits to Sennacherib, 19.
— hinders pacification of Judah, 26 f.
— joins in attack on Jerusalem, 34.
— influenced by Hellenism, 67.
Amon, date of accession, 17.
Amos, Book of, 8.
Andronicus murders Oniah, 52.
Anshan, 29.
Antioch, seat of Seleucid Government, 50–52.
— temple of Τύχη at, 59 f.
Antiochus I, becomes master of Tyre, 38.
Antiochus III takes possession of Palestine, 38.
— welcomed by the Jews, 38, 50, 53.
Antiochus IV (Epiphanes) declares himself King of Syria, 51.
— appoints Jason High Priest, 51.
— appoints Menelaus in place of Jason, 52.
— invades Egypt, 52-54.
— determines on Hellenization of Jerusalem, 55 f.
— στρατηγὸς ἐπὶ τὰ ὅπλα at Athens, 58.
Aphrodite in the Gardens, 57.
Apollonius seizes Jerusalem, 55.
Apries (Hophra), accession of, 25.
Ar, 34.
Aramaic, spoken in Syene, 28.
Armenia, attacked by Phraortes, 29.
Arpad, 17.
Artaxerxes (Longimanus), 34.
Artaxerxes Ochus, 35 f.

Ashdod, Sargon's expedition against, 18.
Asher, not affected by Samaritan schism, 45.
Ashkelon, taken by Sennacherib, 19.
— invaded by Scythians, 24.
Ashur-bani-pal (Asnappar), colonizes Samaria, 23.
— quells revolt in Babylon, 24.
Asshur, 32.
Assideans, see Ḥasidim.
Assouan (Syene), Jewish settlement at, 27 f.
Assyria, ambitious policy of, 10, 12-14.
— Isaiah's teaching concerning, 20 f.
— decline of, 24.
— Cyrus's policy towards, 32.
— name used to denote Seleucid empire, 72.
— expected conversion of, 75.
Astyages, 29.
Athens, the source of Antiochus's innovations at Jerusalem, 56 ff.
Azariah (Azriau), probable identity of, 9 f.

Baal, name used as equivalent of *Zeus*, 59.
Babylon, relations of, with Assyria, 17, 24.
— Jews carried captive to, 26 f.
— opens its gates to Cyrus, 29.
— prophecies relating to, 30 ff.
Baethgen, *Beiträge zur semitischen Religionsgeschichte*, 60 *n*.
Bagoas, governor of Judah, 35.
Bashan, 43-45, 48.
Belsharusur (Belshazzar), 29.
Ben Sira quotes book of Isaiah, 32, 40, 78.
— — reference to the canonical prophets, 41.
Beth Shan (Scythopolis), 24.
Bevan, Prof. A. A., *The Book of Daniel*, 59 *n*.
Bevan, E. R., *Jerusalem under the High Priest*, 66.
— — *House of Seleucus*, 37 *n*, 51 *n*, 53 *n*, 54 *n*, 55, 58 *n*, 59 *n*, 62.
Box, Rev. G. H., *Book of Isaiah*, 4, 35, 36 *n*.
Burkitt, Prof. F. C., 74 *n*.

Cambyses, accession of, 33.
— mentioned in Elephantine papyri, 28.
Cappadocia invaded by the Medes, 29.
Captives carried to Babylon, numbers of, 25.
Carchemish, battle of, 24.
Cheyne, Professor, 2, 35 f., 59 *n*.
Chronicles, 11, 44 f.
Coele-Syria conquered by Alexander, 36.

Confederacy of Palestinian states against Assyria, 18.
Consolatory passages introduced into denunciations, 8.
Cook, Mr. A. B., 58, 61.
Croesus, King of Lydia, 29.
Cyaxares, King of Media, 24.
Cylinder inscriptions of Cyrus, 32 f.
Cyrus succeeds to throne of Media, 29.
— enters Babylon, 29 f.
— policy of, 32 f.
— prophecies relating to, 31 f.

Damascus, alliance with N. Israel, 12 f.
— attacked by Tiglath Pileser, 15 f.
— revolts against Sargon, 17.
— scene of Jonathan's campaign, 69.
Daniel, book of: parallels with book of Isaiah, 37.
— — relation to prophetic literature, 46 f.
— — position in Greek Bible, 79.
Darenberg and Saglio, 71 n.
Darius I, policy of, 33.
David, House of, policy of, 10 f., 34.
Delitzsch, 61 n.
Demetrius I, hostage in Rome, 51.
Demetrius II, relations with the Jews, 68 f.
Deuteronomy, date of, 43.
Dibon invaded by a foe from the desert, 34.
Driver, Prof. S. R., 53 n, 57, 59 n.
Duhm, 2.
Dûr-ilu, 32.

Ebal, 74.
Ecbatana sacked by Cyrus, 29.
Ecclesiastes, Synagogue practice in reading, 8.
Ecclesiasticus, date of translation, 80.
Edom, alliance with Egypt, 18.
— submits to Sennacherib, 19.
— joins in attack on Jerusalem, 34.
— invaded by Bedouin, 34.
— Hasmonaean vengeance on, 67 f.
Egypt, policy of, 16 f.
— war with Assyria, 23 f.
— Jewish refugees settle in, 27 f.
— subdued by Cambyses, 33.
— subdued by Artaxerxes, 36.
— subdued by Alexander, 37.
— Ptolemaic rule in, 38.
— condition of Jews in, 47 f.
— war with Antiochus, 52 ff.
— building of temple in, 64 f.
— expected conversion of, 72 ff.
— gradual reception of the Scriptures, 79 ff.
Ekron deposes Padi, 18.
— captured by Sennacherib, 19.
— assigned to Jonathan, 68.
Elam aids Merodach Baladan, 18.
— alliance with Shamash-shumukin, 24.
— united with Media, 29 f.
Elath, capture of, 12 f.

Elephantine, temple at, 28, 33, 35.
Eliakim, speech of, 28.
Elijah and Elisha, stories of, 8, 45.
Eltekeh, battle of, 19.
Enoch, book of, 47.
Esar-haddon, reign of, 23 f.
Eshnunak, 32.
Euergetes II, reign of, 52 f., 80 f.
Eulacus, regent of Egypt, 52.
Eumenes of Pergamos, 51.
Ezekiel declares the King of Judah's oath of allegiance to be binding, 20.
— prophesies the defeat of Egypt, 29.
— phraseology of, 30.
— foretells ruin of Ammon, &c., 34.
— book of, brought to Palestine, 40 f.
— influence of, in Babylonia, 43, 45.
— referred to, in book of Isaiah, 73 f.
Ezra, book of, reference to Cyrus, 33.
— brings to Palestine scriptures of Babylonian Jews, 40 f.
— influence on the Hebrew Canon, 78 f.

Flood narratives in Genesis, 30.
Frazer, Prof. J. G., 57 n, 58 n, 59 n, 65 n.

Gad, name of Semitic god of fortune, 59 f.
Galilee, invaded by Tiglath Pileser, 15.
— accepts Deuteronomy, 43 f.
— effect of Samaritan schism on, 45, 48.
— Maccabean campaigns in, 67, 69 f.
Gaza, captured by Tiglath Pileser, 15.
— alliance with Egypt, 17.
— receives part of Judaean territory, 19.
Gedaliah, appointed governor of Judah, 26.
— murder of, 26 f.
Gezer, taken by Simon, 69.
Gilead, invaded by Tiglath Pileser, 15.
— accepts Deuteronomic Law, 43 f.
— effect of Samaritan schism on, 45.
— relations with Jerusalem, 48.
— Maccabean campaign in, 67.
Golan, city of refuge, 44.
Gomorrah (see Sodom), 21.

Haggai, book of, how edited, 8.
— perhaps originally joined with Zechariah, 41.
— regards Persian empire as an oppressor, 33.
Hagiographa, date of translation, 81.
Hamath, alliance with Judah, 9 f.
— revolts against Sargon, 17.
Hanno, King of Gaza, 15, 17.
Harpagus, 29.
Harranians, mice sacrificed by, 61.
Harrison, Miss J., *Prolegomena to the Study of Greek Religion*, 57 n, 59 n, 61 n.
Hart, Mr. J. H. A., *Ecclesiasticus in Greek*, 80 f.
Ḥasidîm, 50 ff., 56, 58, 61.
— addressed in Ps. l, 64 f.
— referred to in Isaiah lii. 13–liii, 72.
— altered attitude towards Hellenists, 77.
Hasmonaeans, origin of name, 66.

GENERAL INDEX

Hebrew not understood in Egypt, 28, 47, 74, 79.
Heliodorus conspires against Seleucus IV, 51.
Heliopolis, 64.
Hellenism, spread of, 49 ff., 67, 75.
Hellenization of Jerusalem, 55 f.
Heracles, sacrifice to, 51.
Heroum, description of, 57 f.
Heshbon invaded by Bedouin, 35.
Hezekiah, year of accession, 16 f.
— relations with Assyria, 18 ff.
— reforms of, 20.
— passover in reign of, 44 f.
Historical criticism necessary to supplement literary criticism, 4.
Hophra (Apries) instigates Palestinian states to rebel, 25.
Hosea, book of, 7.
Hoshea, placed on throne by Tiglath Pileser, 15.
— refuses tribute, 16.
Hyrcanus, son of Tobijah, 50.

Imhoof-Blumer und Otto Keller, *Tier- und Pflanzenbilder auf Münzen und Gemmen*, 61.
Immanuel, prophecy of, 13 f., 78.
Isaiah, call of, 9.
— meeting with Ahaz, 13.
— gives his sons symbolical names, 11, 13 f.
— opposes schemes of revolt, 18.
— foretells downfall of Assyria, 20.
Isaiah, book of, nucleus of, 6 ff.
— not quoted by Jeremiah, 6.
— absence of direct attack on superstitions of Isaiah's time, 21.
— regarded as book of national consolation, 22.
— combined with later prophecies, 30 ff., 39 ff.
— quoted by Ben Sira, 78.
— date of, 79 f.
Ishmael murders Gedaliah, 26.
Issus, 36.

Jason (Jeshua), an ardent Hellenizer, 50.
— appointed High Priest, 51.
— deposed in favour of Menelaus, 52.
— attacks Jerusalem, 54, 63.
Jehoiakim takes oath of allegiance to Nebuchadnezzar, 24.
— revolts, 25.
Jeremiah, book of, 8, 40 f.
Jeroboam II, 10.
Jerusalem taken by Nebuchadnezzar, 25.
— burnt by the Chaldeans, 26.
— attacked by Samaritans, 34.
— oppressed by Bagoas, 35.
— influenced by Hellenism, 49-51.
— massacre in, 54 f.
— remodelled by Antiochus Epiphanes, 55 ff., 61 ff.
— regained by the Maccabees, 66.
— surrender of Syrian garrison, 69.
Jeshua, see Jason.

Jezreel, text of Hosea's sermon, 11.
Joash, King of Israel, 10.
Job, book of, 47.
Joel, book of, 41.
Jonah, book of, 39, 41.
Jonathan, campaign in Philistia, 68, 71.
— made High Priest, 68.
— makes terms with Demetrius II, 69.
— put to death by Tryphon, 69.
Joppa, seized by Simon, 69.
Josephus, 35 n, 36, 38, 47, 50 n, 64, 67 n, 80 n.
Josiah, date of accession, 17, 23.
— opposes Pharaoh Necho, 24.
Judah, tributary to N. Israel, 9 f.
— invaded by Syro-Ephraimitic army, 10.
— subject to Sargon, 17.
— invaded by Sennacherib, and deprived of forty-six strong cities, 19.
— subject to Assyria till the death of Josiah, 23 f.
— prophetic teaching concerning, 39.
— antagonistic to Hellenism, 49, 66 f., 77.
Judas, 'blameless priests' chosen by, 75 f.

Kedesh in Naphtali, 43.
Kings, book of, uncertain chronology, 9, 16.
Kittim, 37.
Kosters, 41.

Labashi-Marduk, 29.
Lamentations, Synagogue reading of, 8.
Law, book of, published by Nehemiah, 35, 41, 45 f.
— — translation of, 47 f., 78.
— — attempt to destroy, 75 f.
Lenaeus, regent of Egypt, 52.
Lenormant et de Witte, *Élite des Monuments céramographiques*, 61 n.
Leontopolis, Temple of, 48, 64, 74, 80.
Literary criticism insufficient by itself, 4.
Lydia, 29.
Lysias, general of Antiochus, 66.

Maccabees, 66 ff.
Maher-shalal-hash-baz, 14 f.
Maimonides, 61.
Malachi, teaching of, 39.
Manasseh, reign of, 23.
Manasseh, district of, contains loyal Jews, 45.
Mattaniah (Zedekiah), placed on the throne by Nebuchadnezzar, 25.
Mattathias, 66.
Medeba, invasion of, 34.
Medes, Assyria attacked by, 24.
— united with Persians, 29 f.
Megiddo, battle of, 24.
Memphis, taken by Esarhaddon, 23.
— Jewish refugees settle in, 28.
— seat of Ptolemy Philometor's government, 53 f.
Menelaus appointed High Priest, 52.

GENERAL INDEX

Menelaus carries out the Hellenization of Jerusalem, 55 f., 75 f.
Merodach Baladan, 17 f.
Mê-Turnu, 32.
Micah, quoted as a precedent in time of Jeremiah, 7.
— denounces ruling classes in reign of Hezekiah, 20.
— denounces prophets, 46.
Micaiah, son of Imlah, 11.
Migdol, 28.
Minor Prophets, Synagogue reading of, 8.
Mizpah, residence of Gedaliah, 27.
— reading of the Law at, 76.
Moab, alliance with Egypt, 18.
— makes submission to Sennacherib, 19.
— invasion of, by Bedouin, 34 f.
— hostile to the Jews, 36.
— insignificant Jewish population, 44.
— Maccabean vengeance on, 67 f.
Mond papyri, 27.

Nabonidus, 29.
Nabopolassar, 24.
Nagidos, coins of, 61.
Naphtali receives Deuteronomy, 43 ff.
Nebo, 34.
Nebuchadnezzar, reign of, 24 ff.
— besieges Tyre, 28 f.
Necho, King of Egypt, 24.
Nehemiah, publication of the Law by, 35.
— policy of, 38 f., 44.
— lasting effects of his work, 67.
Nergal-sharezer (Neriglissar), 29.
Nimrim, 35.
Nineveh, fall of, 24.
Noph (Memphis), 28, 53.
North Israel, Kingdom of, relations with Judah, 9, 12.
— — history of, in the reign of Manasseh, 23.

Obadiah, date of, 41.
Olympia Heroum, 57.
Oniah, High Priest, 50 ff.
— murdered at Antioch, 52.
Oniah, Priest of Leontopolis, 48, 64, 74.

Padi, King of Ekron, 18.
Palmyra, Aramaic inscriptions of, 59.
Panion, battle of, 38.
Passover (Hezekiah's), 44 f.
Pathros, 28.
Pausanias' Description of Greece, quoted, 57-61.
Pekah, King of Israel, 15.
Pelusium, 28, 52 ff.
Pentateuch, Septuagint translation of, 48, 79.
Persia, united with Media, 29.
— attitude of prophets towards, 33.
— supposed Jewish revolt against, 35.
Pharaoh, name still used in second century A.D., 54 n.
Pharisees, denounced in the Gospels, 46.

Philippeum, begun by Philip of Macedon, 58.
Philistia, alliances with, 12, 18.
— Scythian invasion of, 24.
— Hellenization of, 59 f., 67.
— Maccabean campaign in, 67 ff., 71.
Phoenicia, subdued by Sennacherib, 18 f.
— tributary to Esarhaddon, 23.
— subdued by Alexander, 37.
Phraortes, King of Media, 29.
Pinches, *The Old Testament in the Light of the Historical Records of Assyria and Babylonia*, 32 n.
Pindar, 60.
Prophets, character of, 46.
Prophets, Canon of the, 41 f., 78 ff.
Psalms, parallels with book of Isaiah, 86 f.
Psammetichus I, 24.
Psammetichus II, 25.
Ptolemais, Jonathan seized at, 69.
Ptolemy (Soter) transfers Jews to Egypt, 38, 47.
Ptolemy Euergetes I, 80.
Ptolemy Euergetes II, 52 ff., 80 f.
Ptolemy Philadelphus, 80.
Ptolemy Philometor, 52, 54, 64.
Ptolemy Philopator, 81.
Ptolemy Physcon, 81.

Qutû, 32.

Ramoth in Gilead, 44.
Raphiah, battle of, 17.
Reisch, 60 n.
Reuben, 44.
Riblah, 25.
Rome compels Antiochus to evacuate Egypt, 54.
Roscher, *Lexikon der Griechischen und Römischen Mythologie*, 60 n.

Sacrificial worship, yearning for, 64.
Samaria taken by Sargon, 16.
Samaria, province of, colonized, 23, 28.
— — accepts Deuteronomic law, 43 f.
— — quarrels with Judah, 34 f.
Sanctuary, One, law of, 43 f., 48, 74.
Sardis, taken by Cyrus, 29.
Sargon, reign of, 16 ff.
Schechter, Dr., 3.
Schrader, 9 n.
Scribes, origin of, 46.
— influence of, 76 f.
Scriptures, destruction of, 56, 75 f.
— translation of, 79 ff.
Scythians, 24.
Scythopolis, 24.
Seleucus IV, 50 f.
Sennacherib, reign of, 17 ff.
Septuagint, origin of, 47 f.
— date of, 79 ff.
Shalmaneser, 16.
Shamash-shumukin, 24.
Sharon, Plain of, 70.
Shear-jashub, meaning of, 10 f.

GENERAL INDEX

Shebna, 28.
Shechem, chief sanctuary of Samaria, 43, 56.
Shelley's imitation of the National Anthem, 3.
Sibylline Oracles, 53.
Sidon, destroyed by Artaxerxes, 36.
— opens its gates to Alexander, 37.
Siloam, 15.
Simon, son of Oniah, High Priesthood of, 45, 48.
Simon Maccabeus appointed Governor of Palestine, 69.
— — acknowledged High Priest, 70.
— — High Priesthood of, 71 ff.
Simyra, 17.
Sippar, 29.
Skinner, Dr., *Commentary on Isaiah*, 60.
Smith, Robertson, 57 *n*, 61 *n*.
Sodom, variable use of name, 21.
Superstitions, absence of direct attack on, in genuine Isaiah, 21.
Susa, 29, 32.
Syene, 27.
Synagogues, origin of, 45 f.
— importance of, 76 f.

Tahpanhes (Tel Defenneh), 28.
Tanis (Zoan), 53.
Tarshish, ships of, 37, 69.
Tell Ta'annek, 57.
Temple (of Jerusalem) plundered by Nebuchadnezzar, 25.
— wealth of, in second century B.C., 48 f.

Temple (of Jerusalem), injured in struggle between Jason and Menelaus, 54.
— desecrated by Antiochus Epiphanes, 55 ff.
— condition of, in 165 B.C., 61 ff.
— regained by the Maccabees, 66.
Temple of Leontopolis, 48, 64, 74, 80.
Tiglath Pileser III, 9 f., 15, 44.
Tigris, 32.
Tirhakah, 18.
Tobiah, the sons of, 38, 53.
Tobijah, father of Hyrcanus, 50.
Tryphon, general of Alexander Balas, 69.
Tyre besieged by Nebuchadnezzar, 28.
— prophecy on, 37 f.
— games at, 51.

Uzziah, probable identification with Azriau of Yaudi, 9 f.

Wellhausen, 63 *n*.
Winckler, 9.

Zamban, 32.
Zebulon, 44 f.
Zechariah, attitude of, towards Persia, 33.
— deprecates fortification of Jerusalem, 34.
Zedekiah, revolt of, 25.
Zerubbabel appointed Governor of Judah, 33 f.
Zeus, represented in Hebrew and Aramaic by Baal, 55 f.
Zion fortified by Antiochus, 55.
Zoan (Tanis), 53.

PASSAGES OF SCRIPTURE QUOTED OR REFERRED TO

	PAGE
GENESIS:	
vii. 2, 8	3 n.
EXODUS:	
vii. 14–21	54 n.
xx. 25	58
xxi. 32	51 n.
NUMBERS:	
xxiv. 24	37
DEUTERONOMY:	
iv. 43	44
vi. 9	57
xvi. 21	62
xviii. 11	59
xix.	43
xxiii. 3	27 n.
xxvii.	74 n.
xxxiii. 6	44
JOSHUA:	
xi. 17	59
xii. 7	59
xiii. 5	59
xv. 37	59
xx. 8	44
xxi. 27, 38	44
xxi. 32	43
xxii.	74 n.
1 KINGS:	
v.	37
xi. 29 ff.	41
xviii. 31	41
xix. 16	32 n.
xxii. 28	11
2 KINGS:	
xv. 29	15
xvi. 5	12
xviii. 2	16
xviii. 13	17
xx. 6	17
xxiv. 2, 12, 14, 16	25
xxiv. 13	33
xxv. 3	26
xxv. 6	25
xxv. 8, 25	27
1 CHRONICLES:	
ix. 29	60 n.
2 CHRONICLES:	
xxviii. 18	18 n.
xxx.	44
EZRA:	
i.	32
iv. 2, 10	23
vi. 22	72 n.
NEHEMIAH:	
i. 3	63
xiii.	44

	PAGE
JOB:	
vii. 3	60 n.
PSALMS:	
xxii. 1	66
xlii.	64 n.
xliii.	64 n.
xliv. 22	65
xlvi. 4	73 n.
l.	64
lx.	36
lx. 8	68 n.
lxi. 8	60 n.
lxiii.	64
lxix. 28	77 n.
lxxiv. 4 ff.	63
lxxviii. 12, 43	53
lxxxiii.	36, 68 n.
lxxxiii. 10	68 n.
lxxxvii.	38
cv. 15	32 n.
ISAIAH:	
i. 4 ff.	66 n.
i. 7–9	20
i. 10–17	20
i. 11–14	21
i. 21–23	20
i. 29	57
ii. 3	73 n.
ii. 6 f.	12
iii. 6–9	20
iii. 14, 15	20
v. 8–10	20
v. 26–30	18
vi. 13	11
vii. 1–7	12
vii. 2	8
vii. 3	10
vii. 8	23
vii. 13	12
viii. 7 ff.	15 n.
viii. 16, 17	6
ix. 1–7	71, 78
ix. 9 ff.	16
ix. 13 ff.	20
x. 6	15 n.
x. 21	3
x. 22	11
x. 28–32	18
xi. 1	26, 71 n.
xi. 6	75 n.
xi. 9	75
xi. 14	68
xi. 15	73 n.
xi. 16	72 n.
xiii.	30, 40

PASSAGES OF SCRIPTURE QUOTED, ETC.

Isaiah (continued):	PAGE
xiv.	30, 40
xiv. 29 f.	18 n.
xv.	34, 35
xvi.	34, 35
xix. 1–15	53, 54
xix. 18	74 n.
xix. 23 ff.	72 n.
xx. 1.	18
xxi. 1–10	30, 40
xxi. 11 ff.	34
xxii. 15–23	20
xxiii.	37
xxiii. 17	38
xxiv.—xxvii.	35, 36, 78
xxv. 6	74 n.
xxv. 7	70 n.
xxviii. 7–22	20
xxx.	65
xxxi.	65
xxxii. 1 f.	71 n.
xxxiii. 13–24	73
xxxiii. 17	71 n.
xxxiii. 18	70 n.
xxxiv.	68
xxxviii. 5	17
xxxix. 7.	18
xl—xlviii.	30
xl. 1–11	31
xl—lxvi.	39
xl. 3 ff.	73
xli. 1–7	32
xlii. 4	69 n.
xliv. 24—xlv. 7	31
xlvi. 1, 2	31, 32
xlvii.	31, 32
xlviii. 20	32
xlix. 6	72 n, 73 n.
lii. 13—liii.	72
liii.	72 n.
lv. 7	77 n.
lvi. 9—lvii. 13	56
lix. 16	66 n.
lx. 9	69 n.
lx. 20	75 n.
lx. 22	70 n.
lxi. 1	31, 40
lxiii. 1 ff.	72 n.
lxiii. 1–6	67
lxiii. 4 ff.	78 n.
lxiv. 10, 11	63
lxv. 3	61, 62
lxv. 4, 11	59
lxv. 17	75
lxv. 25	75 n.
lxvi. 1 ff.	65
lxvi. 5	66
lxvi. 6	67 n.
lxvi. 7	70 n.
lxvi. 17	57, 60
lxvi. 22–24	74 n.

Jeremiah:	
vii. 21	21
xxiii. 5 ff.	26 n.
xxiii. 14	26 n.
xxv.	25

Jeremiah (continued):	PAGE
xl.	25, 27
xli.	25
xli. 5	63 n.
xliv.	28
xlvi.	28
l.	30
li.	30
lii. 28	25
lii. 29	26
lii. 30	27

Ezekiel:	
xvi.	57 n.
xvii. 13–16	25
xvii. 15, 16	20
xxi. 18 ff.	26
xxv.	27 n.
xxvi.	29
xxix. 17–20	29
xxx. 6	28
xlvii.	73

Daniel:	
i. 5, 10, 11	60 n.
iii. 17	65
viii. 23	53
xi. 30	37

Hosea:	
v. 10	12 n.

Joel:	
iii. 11, 18	78 n.

Jonah:	
ii. 1	60 n.
iv. 6–8	60 n.

Micah:	
iii.	46
vi.	21

Haggai:	
ii. 3	63 n.
ii. 6–8	33

Zechariah:	
i. 12	33 n.
ii. 6, 7	32 n.
iii. 8	26 n.
vi. 12	26 n.
ix—xiv	36
ix. 5 ff.	60 n.
ix. 5–7	68
ix. 6	56 n.
ix. 9	71 n.
ix. 12	32
xi.	50 n.
xi. 15–17	56 n.
xiii. 2–6	46
xiii. 7	77 n.
xiv.	73
xiv. 2	73
xiv. 4	77 n.
xiv. 6, 7	75 n.
xiv. 16–19	74 n.
xiv. 18	48

Malachi:	
iv. 2	68 n.

Ecclesiasticus:	
i. 1 f.	63 n.
i. 1–5	48
xi. 25–28	65 n.

ECCLESIASTICUS (*continued*):
	PAGE
xlviii. 22 ff.	40, 78 n.
xlviii. 24	32

1 MACCABEES:
	PAGE
i. 1	37
i. 15	52 n.
i. 21 ff.	62
i. 22	63
i. 54	55 n, 59 n.
i. 56 f.	75 n.
ii. 29 ff.	65 n, 72 n.
iii. 45	62 n.
iii. 48	76 n.
iii. 51	75 n.
iv. 38	54 n, 61
iv. 42	75 n.
v. 3, 65	67

1 MACCABEES (*continued*):
	PAGE
v. 4 ff., 28	67 n.
vii. 13, 14	76 n.
xi. 59	69 n.
xiii. 41, 51	69 n.
xiv. 41	70 n.
xiv. 41, 46	76 n.

2 MACCABEES:
	PAGE
i. 8	54 n, 63 n.
iii. 11	50 n.
iv. 18–20	57 n.
iv. 37	53 n.
vi. 1	56 n.
viii. 33	54 n, 63
x. 18 ff.	67 n.

S. LUKE:
	PAGE
iv. 18, 19	32

www.ingramcontent.com/pod-product-compliance
Lightning Source LLC
Chambersburg PA
CBHW070703100426
42735CB00039B/2780